Tales of Old H

Tales of
Old Hampshire

Cecilia Millson

With illustrations by Don Osmond

COUNTRYSIDE BOOKS
NEWBURY, BERKSHIRE

ISBN 0 905392 05 1

Designed by Mon Mohan

Produced through MRM (Print Consultants) Ltd., Reading
Printed in Great Britain by J.W. Arrowsmith Ltd., Bristol

To Lucy, Arabella
and Alexandra

Contents

HANTSHIRE – The map overleaf is by John Speede and shows the county as it was in the late sixteenth century.

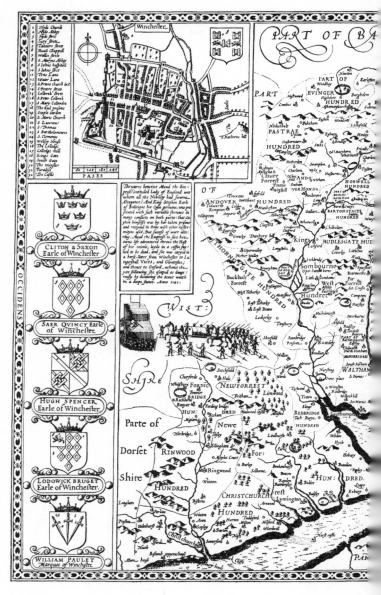

The Loss of the Mary Rose

Portsmouth has seen more of British naval history in the making than any other port of England. Her harbour has been the home of countless warships whose very names send patriotic blood coursing through the veins. Nelson's great ship *Victory* remains there, the epitome of a proud tradition of mastery of the seas. For four hundred and thirty seven years an equally proud but tragic warship, the *Mary Rose*, lay a little off shore in what was thought to be her last resting place. This ship, pride of the expanding navy of King Henry VIII and one of the most formidable fighting vessels of her day, lay buried in silt and mud, together with at least 400 of her crew, 40 feet beneath the spot where she capsized and sank in 1545.

King Henry himself, watching from Southsea Castle at the head of his army, could only look on horrified as the mighty ship disappeared beneath the waters of the Solent. But from this disaster which claimed so many lives has now come some good fortune. The centuries dealt kindly with the *Mary Rose*. Preserved by the mud into which she sank over four hundred years ago, she lay more or less intact to await the time when she was lifted out of the slime and taken ashore to eventually become the centrepiece of a major maritime museum at Portsmouth.

When the young and ambitious Henry VIII came to the throne in 1509 he inherited from his father Henry VII a small but growing fleet. He knew that he must continue to increase the English navy both in terms of its numbers of ships and their fighting capabilites. England was by no means secure from her neighbours on the continent and sea power would be equally as vital as land power. His programme of naval rearmament began almost as soon as he ascended the throne with the laying down of two new battleships or "carracks" at Portsmouth. One was to be called *Peter Pomegranate* and the other was to be named after his sister – the *Mary Rose*. Both were to be among the most modern warships in the then known world.

The *Mary Rose* was launched in 1511 and it is recorded that Henry paid for her to be sailed up to the Thames in order to have her fitted out with new guns, some of which he had specially commissioned from leading European gunmakers. We do not know what she looked like at this time but she was a 600-ton ship, carried 78 guns of various sizes, and was crewed by 120 sailors, 20 gunners, 2 pilots, 5 trumpeters, and 36 servants. She also carried 251 pikemen and archers. Her fighting capabilities were soon put to the test during the war with France in 1512. She acquitted herself well and Sir Edward Howard, the Commander of the English fleet, used her as his flagship. He described her in a letter to Henry as "your good ship, the flower I trow of all ships that ever sailed".

With the ending of the war in 1514 the *Mary Rose* was put into reserve. Little was then heard of her until 1536 when she was completely refitted. Her tonnage was uprated to 700 tons and she was fitted with 91 guns, including some of the heaviest and most modern then in existence. Her crew remained at around 400 men. The only existing painting of her was done immediately after the refit and shows her proud and sinister, flags flying from her masts, guns bristling from her sides.

It is possible that it was at this time that her main construction was altered from clinker to carvel type. That is, her hull sides were changed from overlapping planks to a smooth planking fastened to heavy frames with oak-tree nails which gave considerable extra strength to the whole ship. It also allowed heavy guns to be placed on gun decks nearer to the water line which could fire broadside into enemy ships. Watertight hatches by each gun could be securely closed when the ship was under way or if the sea was choppy. Not only was firepower much increased by this but the weight of the guns lower down in the ship gave increased buoyancy. This allowed extra men and guns to be placed in the big high castles at the bow and stern of the ship without the danger of its becoming top-heavy and capsizing. These men aloft were still vital in naval warfare as, after an enemy ship had been rammed or otherwise secured, a vicious hail of arrows could be fired down from the castles onto her decks and, when sufficient loss had been inflicted, pikemen would board the enemy to capture the ship and kill any members of her crew still alive. No quarter was given. There was no room or manpower to spare for holding prisoners and besides they might well later mount a surprise counter-attack on their captors.

The *Mary Rose* was therefore a queen on the English naval chessboard when in 1545 Francis I of France declared war on Henry and made ready a vast fleet with which to invade the south coast. 235 ships with 30,000 men sailed from the Seine Estuary and made for Portsmouth where they hoped to destroy the English fleet. It is interesting to note that this little-talked-of armada was actually bigger by nearly 100 ships than the famous Spanish Armada in 1588.

Henry, immediately he learned what was happening, set about organising a formidable reception committee and went down to Portsmouth to personally take control of the English forces. He hastened the fitting out of the ships which lay in the harbour, and saw with satisfaction the huge army which Charles Brandon, Duke of Suffolk, had assembled on Southsea Common.

All was, therefore, in readiness for an expected attack when the French armada, under the command of Admiral Claude d'Annebault, was sighted off the north-east corner of the Isle of Wight on July 19th, 1545.

The Lord High Admiral, Viscount Lisle, commanded the English fleet from his flagship *Henry Grace à Dieu*, and the *Mary Rose* flew the flag of the newly-appointed Vice-Admiral, Sir George Carew. Her captain was Roger Grenville.

Sir Peter Carew, the younger brother of Sir George, has left an account of that fateful day. He relates how the King conducted a kind of working lunch with his senior officers on board his flagship. Henry briefed his Admirals, and followed this with a stormy interview with the French Ambassador, then he asked for news of the enemy. Sir Peter rose from the table and went aloft. He reported that four ships were approaching which he first thought were merchantmen, but he soon realised that they were the vanguard of the French fleet.

The Vice-Admiral then returned to the *Mary Rose* and Portsmouth harbour became full of activity as sails were hoisted and the ships all moved out into the Solent for battle, but the wind was so still that movement was necessarily slow. Four French galleys, oar-powered and ideal for calm weather, moved forward and exchanged shots with *Henry Grace à Dieu*. Then the breeze increased, favouring the English ships, and they released more sails to take advantage of it and drive forward towards the French.

At that point, to everyone's horror, the *Mary Rose* was seen to heel. The Commander of the *Mathew Gonson* drew his ship alongside her and called out, asking what was amiss, to which Sir George shouted back "I have the sort of knaves I cannot rule". Very quickly the list became more acute as water poured in through her open gun ports only 16 inches above the waterline. The *Mary Rose* sank rapidly. Packed closely inside their solid wooden fortress, and weighed down with armour, her crew had little chance of escape from the massive inrush of water. Only 40 were rescued out of the 700 men who Sir Peter Carew recorded as being on board. If his figure is correct the overloading from her normal complement of just over 400 men may well have contributed to the tragedy.

In the light of Sir George's remark about his "unruly knaves" some thought that the loss was due to the insubordination and negligence of her crew. Others put forward the theory that, with the gun ports only 16 inches above the water-line, they took in water as the ship, overheavy with guns and men, swayed when she turned for action. The French had yet another explanation. They said that the *Mary Rose* had been hit by cannon fire from their guns. This was refuted by the eyewitnesses who included the King and the poor wife of Sir George Carew, who was comforted by Henry as she watched her husband's ship go down, and heard the cries of the drowning sailors.

Within two weeks of the event plans were formulated for the

salvage of the wreck, and Venetian salvors were summoned to Portsmouth with their equipment which was recognised as the best available at that period. Unfortunately, the attempt was unsuccessful, only the sails and the yards were recovered. Over the next four years some guns were salvaged but that was all. She lay in six fathoms of water at low tide so that her masts could be seen above sea level as late as the seventeenth century, but as the years passed the *Mary Rose* became but a memory.

However, that memory was revived in 1836 when two divers, John and Charles Deane, were called upon to work on the wreck of the *Royal George* which had sunk at Spithead in 1782. Local fishermen were troubled by the fact that their lines caught on an underwater obstruction and they asked the two brothers to investigate for them. The Deanes dived at the spot indicated and established the remains of the *Mary Rose* as the cause of the trouble.

Salvage work was started and many objects were recovered – 4 bronze guns, 20 iron guns, wooden utensils, long bows, pottery. Some articles were preserved for display at the Southsea Castle Museum; all were recorded, but much of the salvaged material was made into souvenirs, and some was sold by auction in Portsmouth. The *Mary Rose* was then forgotten again.

In 1965 a new search for the ship was made, and through the determined work of Alexander McKee and members of the Southsea Branch of the British Sub-Aqua Club, the wreck was once again located. This time survey and systematic excavation rather than salvage were the aims of the divers. Salvaged objects were not made into souvenirs! Instead careful recording and conservation of all recovered artifacts are being carried out by a team of experts in the laboratory of the Portsmouth City Museum. Many finds have been made which reveal important sidelights on sixteenth century life.

An elegant pewter wine flagon, plates bearing the crest and initials of George Carew, bones of venison and pork, wild damson and plum stones, bring the crew's last luncheon vividly to life, whilst a games board, a domino, and early musical instruments prove that entertainment was not forgotten amid the grim preparations for war.

15

A naval surgeon-barber has left the imprint of his fingers on a jar of ointment found in a box which also contains his complete set of instruments. The sailors whom he treated have left their personal belongings behind, a bosun's whistle, a braided jerkin, leather boots and shoes, a hand knitted stocking and a felt hat are but some of the articles of clothing found among the wreckage. Human bones, a reminder of the tragic end of a fine ship and her gallant crew, have been buried with honour in the port from which the ship sailed so many centuries ago.

In January 1979 The Mary Rose Trust was inaugurated to administer and finance the expanding underwater excavations and the final lifting and recovery of the ship's hull. A team of more than 200 volunteer divers, archaeologists, historians, and technical experts worked from a base ship, the lifting vessel, Sleipner, which was involved in the operation to raise the seventeenth century Swedish ship *Wasa* in Stockholm.

In June 1982 a steel lifting frame was positioned over the hull and attached to its ancient timbers which were strengthened to take the strain of the proposed transfer into a supporting cradle. By a very complex underwater operation the hull was lowered into the cradle and cushioned by a pliable mattress of air and water bags.

At three minutes past nine on the cold, misty morning of Monday, October 11th, 1982, the first timbers of the Mary Rose came into view, anxiously watched by the team who had worked so well and for so long to bring this project to a successful conclusion. Not until the precious burden was safely lowered on to the waiting barge did anyone dare to relax.

As the huge barge made its way slowly to Portsmouth Dockyard all England, and overseas friends who had given support to the undertaking, rejoiced that the raising of the *Mary Rose* had been successful.

Today, the starboard half of the great hull stands erect once again, and the task of refitting the salvaged interior timbers has commenced. In the Exhibition Hall the display of artefacts provides a valuable insight into Tudor life.

Visitors come in their thousands. In his proudest moments Henry VIII could never have imagined that such interest would one day be displayed in his fair *Mary Rose*.

Smuggler's Tales

SINCE the beginning of civilization it has only needed the levying of a tax by rulers of men for their subjects to contrive ways to avoid paying it. Import and export duties have always been unpopular, and remain so to this day, and many a cargo has been off loaded, or collected, from some secret place to avoid the payment of duty on it.

Likewise, when a ban is placed on an undesirable commodity, such as harmful drugs, it is a signal for some people to start handling it dishonestly, so that they can make a handsome profit.

Threats of imprisonment, the levying of fines, or, in olden times, fears of deportation and the death penalty, have not deterred the really hardened smugglers from pursuing their disreputable but lucrative occupation.

More often than not, in bygone days, it was sheer necessity which drove seafaring men into the smuggling trade. A bad fishing season would tempt them to carry something more profitable than a few fish in their almost empty boats, and their knowledge of deep caves and well-wooded coves were invaluable when questionable cargoes had to be landed without catching the attention of legal authority.

There were willing hands to carry the goods ashore, and to transport them to rendezvous where customers were waiting to buy tax free merchandise. But once involved, it became difficult for men to leave the dangerous trade, for the fear of betrayal frequently made their comrades vicious towards any who seemed likely to desert the gang to return to a more honest way of life. Some gangs were highly organised by clever leaders who operated in the background leaving rougher men to do the actual work, and they were forces to be reckoned with if they clashed with the law. Excisemen were brave indeed to tackle such men on rugged clifftops, or along dark forest paths.

There were a few young men, probably sons of the local gentry who, from sheer high spirits, viewed a night's run with the village smugglers as good sport; there were certainly those in high places who turned a blind eye to a nocturnal train of pack-horses, and refused to listen to muffled sounds, as long as a keg of tax-free brandy found its way to their cellars, or a parcel of tobacco was left in a concealed cranny. A lady was pleased to wear a gown of fine silk or a shawl of French lace at a party, and a dish of highly expensive tea was always enjoyed providing nobody suspected that these luxurious wares had been left by those who rode through the night. All too frequently good horses were "borrowed" from the stables of the gentry and returned in the morning with a cask of brandy to pay for their hire.

Smuggling was rife in Hampshire and the Isle of Wight. Being situated near to the Continent, a two-way run could be operated. As far back as 1394 the Rector of Freshwater on the Island was summoned for smuggling English wool to France and so cheating King Richard II of his dues.

Nearby Blackgang Chine is said to derive its name from a gang of smugglers who operated along the coastline, where casks of French wine and brandy were landed in the deep inlets and convenient caves.

During the eighteenth and nineteenth centuries the trade increased, and there were very few villages which were not involved, either on the Island or along the Hampshire coast. Casks of brandy were conveyed across the Channel in false-bottomed boats, and swags of tobacco were hidden in coils of tarred hemp. When the cargoes were unloaded they were left in hiding-places until pack-horses could be brought to collect them. Some were hidden in farmyard ricks, others in the cellars of cottages, inns, or lonely houses. Even the square-topped table tombs in the churchyards were used as places of concealment.

Stories of ghostly figures kept the inquisitive away, and flashing lights were sufficient to start stories of haunted houses. The hoot of an owl was just as likely to be a smuggler's signal rather than the true call of the nocturnal bird. It was a brave man who would venture too near a haunted place to verify if it were ethereal wraiths or stalwart smugglers who moved in the shadows.

In the New Forest the table tombs in the lonely churchyard at Boldre made ideal hiding-places for casks of brandy, as they reached the first stage of their journey through the forest after being landed at Lymington. The next call along the "Smugglers' Way", as the route was known, was at the village of Sway where there were large cellars not only in Sway House Inn and the cottages, but in Sway House itself where there was reputed to be a passage running underground for a length of four miles, from the house to the coast.

Further along the "Way" an old woman from Burley, by the name of Lovey Warne, would walk to a hill at Picket Post if the excisemen were near at hand. Her red cloak could be clearly seen as she trudged up the hill, apparently going about her lawful business, but in reality giving a clear warning of impending danger.

The customs officer, or exciseman, was not a popular local figure. At nearby Ringwood, in January 1783, the exciseman heard of a smugglers' depot in Burley and took some of his men with him to investigate the place. He found that the rumours were correct and ordered the men to seize the contraband goods. But news of the raid spread quickly through the forest, horses were saddled, and soon there was a large band of irate smugglers on the trail of the excisemen. When the latter turned to face their pursuers and saw they were hopelessly out-numbered, they dropped the haul and fled, leaving their officer to uphold the law on his own. He was severely injured by the smugglers who left him by the roadside as they made off into the forest with their reclaimed booty. The exciseman recovered eventually but he did not forget that day for many a year.

Another incident occurred at Poole (then a part of Hampshire) when a large quantity of tea, which was highly taxed, was confiscated and placed in the Customs House. The smugglers boldly stormed the building and recovered their hoard. The tea was never seen again – by the customs officers.

Poole appears to have been a popular place for the landing of tea, for there is another story concerning a Captain Diamond who had collected an illicit load and was taking it to Whitsbury when he realised that he was being followed by excisemen. He promptly enlisted the help of a sympathetic farmer who hid the tea under a load of hay so that Captain Diamond was quite empty handed when the excisemen searched him.

Hiding-places for contraband goods were numerous, and all of them demonstrated a remarkable imagination by the Hampshire smugglers. Soberton churchyard boasts a dummy vault near the chancel door which provided useful cover. It probably made a very convenient half-way house for the bundles of silk and lace, and the kegs of brandy, which were taken from Portsmouth to a depot at Medstead, just south of Alton.

One clever smuggler and his family hurriedly wrapped silk and lace around their bodies and covered the precious finery with their own rough clothes when a signal was given that excisemen were in their village.

On the Isle of Wight it was a mother of a new-born baby who saved the day. When excisemen arrived to search the cottage they nearly ransacked the place to find hidden cupboards and loose floorboards, but they hesitated to disturb the young mother and her baby. It was a lucky day for her husband as the contraband was hidden under the bed clothes.

Word was soon passed if danger was around and it was not only the villagers who were on the side of the lawbreakers. At Ropley the local magistrate is said to have entertained the excisemen in his house while a messenger was sent to warn the smugglers that a search was to be made in the cottage where their contraband was hidden.

Sailors used to bring ashore the dirty washing from their ships in large wicker baskets and the cry was often heard, "Has the washing come in yet?" But the words had a double meaning, for frequently the baskets contained contraband amongst the dirty clothes. One sailor had a very uncomfortable time as he was joined by a customs officer who walked along the quayside with him – a friendly gesture which was not appreciated by the sailor, whose load was far heavier than it looked. He longed to put it down and enjoy a brief rest, but he dare not show his fatigue and struggled manfully with it until the officer had bade him goodbye, quite unaware how near he had been to making a good arrest.

The nineteenth century saw a great improvement in the efficiency of the coastguard service, and this heralded the end of the old style gangs of free-traders. They are regarded today with romantic indulgence, but most were dangerous men who stopped at nothing to ensure the success of their nefarious trade. They used, as do professional smugglers today, part-time or amateur smugglers who helped them from necessity, greed, dislike of authority, and a variety of motives including the sheer love of risk and danger.

In the present day, the customs officers are still on the alert to find merchandise in hidden compartments, or amongst seemingly innocent luggage as travellers pass through the ports, and, still, people who live otherwise blameless lives boast to their friends if they manage to evade duty on cigarettes and bottles of spirit. Do they see themselves as descendents of the swashbuckling smugglers who hid their "baccy" and their brandy in lonely churchyard tombs?

Cricket
at Hambledon

THE BISHOP OF WINCHESTER was granted the right to hold two fairs in Hambledon by James I in 1612, and the toll paid to the Lord of the Manor for the setting up of the booths was a broad half-penny. This custom gave the name to the windswept down high above the village, but as the country folk flocked to their fairs they little thought that their Broadhalfpenny Down would become known to cricket lovers all over the world.

Although cricket was played earlier in other parts of England, notably Kent and Sussex, it is Hambledon that has become known as "the cradle of cricket" because of the success of its village club which between the years 1772 and 1781 won twenty-nine of the fifty-one matches it played against England teams.

The most memorable match was played for 1,000 guineas on June 18th, 1777, and was won by the Hambledon Club by an innings and 168 runs. Runs, which were only counted for the side and not for the individual, were notched up on a stick.

The team must have been a joy to behold as it met in the Bat and Ball Inn before the match. The players wore sky blue coats, with velvet collars and buttons embossed with the letters C.C., white shirts and breeches, stockings, buckle shoes, and gold laced tricorne hats which were exchanged for dark velvet caps when the men went out to play. They also discarded their fine coats.

It was the leadership of the landlord of the inn, Richard Nyren, which contributed to the outstanding success of the Club. He had been tutored in cricket by Richard Newland of Sussex and passed on his knowledge of the game to his team. He became its captain, secretary, and groundsman and, above all, was a well-liked and respected man whose decisions on the rules of cricket were accepted not only by his own players but by the leading cricketers of the late eighteenth century.

The matches played on the down attracted huge crowds as Hampshire people came to cheer the village team against the England players. Favourite batsmen were William Beldham (Silver Billie as he was called) and John Small; while David Harris was a bowler whose balls had such a peculiar curl that they could grind a man's finger against the bat. These were the type of men who laid the foundations of English village cricket.

In 1782 Richard Nyren moved to the George Hotel in the village and the club moved to Windmill Down, but with the formation of the Marylebone Cricket Club in 1787 the control and administration of the game slowly passed from Hambledon to Lords, the cricket ground started by Thomas Lord with the support of the Earl of Winchelsea and the Honourable Colonel Lennox, which became the headquarters of the M.C.C.

Richard Nyren left Hambledon in 1791. It was a sad day for the local club. In 1832 the famous captain's son, John Nyren, wrote of his departure in his book *The Young Cricketer's Tutor* and stated, "when Richard Nyren left Hambledon the club broke up and never resumed from that day. The heart and the right arm were gone."

Many mementoes of the Club are preserved at the Bat and Ball Inn which still stands on Broadhalfpenny Down. There is a cricket bat presented to Richard Nyren which is inscribed, "From Old Friends, 'Bat and Ball' Hambledon, Sept: 4th, 1791". William Beldham, in his smock and top hat, looks down from the wall on the room from which he went out to bat and make his "brilliant runs all over the ground", to quote John Nyren. Immediately opposite the inn there is a granite obelisk inscribed with two bats, a ball, and stumps, and the dates 1750–87. This memorial to the famous club, and the pitch on which it played its greatest games, was unveiled before a crowd of 5,000 people in 1908 when a commemorative match was played there after an interval of over one hundred years.

The Bay of Death

CHALE BAY on the south-eastern corner of the Isle of Wight is a place of great beauty. The tall cliffs are cut by deep chasms where streams have tumbled down since time immemorial, and rocks that have fallen in the process lie strewn along the beaches.

In the sunshine of a summer's day the bay seems a haven of peace, but when sudden mists swirl across the waters and a strong inshore current pulls unwary navigators and their ships towards those treacherous rocks, it becomes a nightmare for those who sail the sea.

On a winter's night in the year 1314, a storm-tossed ship was caught in that dreaded current and was swept on to Atherfield Ledge at the northerly end of the bay. It was one of a fleet of vessels which had been chartered by the merchants of Acquitaine, a territorial possession of King Edward II, to carry a consignment of white wine to England.

By good fortune, the shipwrecked sailors managed to scramble ashore. When the storm subsided they returned to the stricken ship and carried the casks of wine from the hold. They salvaged one hundred and seventy-four casks but, instead of waiting for rescue by a sister ship, they decided to sell the wine to any Islanders who could afford to pay the price they demanded for the stolen goods.

Walter de Godeton, who held land in the manor of Chale, bought fifty-three casks and no doubt he congratulated himself

25

on buying some cheap wine, but he was to pay dearly for that bargain.

The merchants were furious when they learned what had happened to their cargo but they decided that it was of little use to trace and charge the sailors. Instead, they turned their attention to the Islanders who had bought the wine.

Walter de Godeton was evidently one of the worst offenders for not only was he fined 227½ marks (about £20,000) in the civil courts but his case was taken further by the religious house in Picardy that owned the wine. The matter was placed before the ecclesiastical courts of Rome and the culprit was admonished for his dishonest dealings, and ordered to build and endow a lighthouse and an oratory on the downs above the bay.

It seems that there was already a hermitage on the site for a Walter de Langstrell lived there in 1312. Perhaps he tried to help those in distress from the sea. He must have watched the building of the lighthouse with great interest. This and the oratory beside it were provided for a monk who was required to say prayers for the souls of those lost at sea, and also to act as lighthouse keeper.

It must have been a lonely life on that desolate clifftop as the monk went about his religious duties, and then climbed the stairs to tend the beacon, which shone from eight oblong slits at the top of an octagonal tower.

It burned until the Reformation in the early sixteenth century when the small revenues were sequestered and the monk could not be supported. His prayers, and the light, were no longer at the service of the men who sailed in those treacherous waters, and over three hundred years were to elapse before the light shone again.

During that time the bay became known as "the Bay of Death" as ship after ship perished in its depths.

Between 1746 and 1808 there were sixty wrecks recorded, and on one disastrous night in 1757, fifteen vessels were tossed on to the dangerous rock-strewn shore.

Inevitably there were some who waited to enrich themselves

from the misfortunes of others. The cargoes from the wrecks were looted almost as soon as they were washed ashore. However, on one occasion disaster befell those who dragged some casks from the waves. When it was realised that they contained rum, the greedy men could not wait until their booty was carried inshore. They opened the casks and drank the liquor on the beach. As one by one they fell down in a drunken stupor the incoming tide washed over them and some were drowned before their more sober companions could pull them to safety.

Eventually the Trinity House Board decided that something must be done to try to prevent the wrecks. In 1785 the old lighthouse was repaired and the light rekindled while a new house was built beside it. The work was never finished as it was discovered that the light was useless in the mists and fogs. Only in the nineteenth century was a new site chosen, 136 feet above the sea at St. Catherine's point, and at last a light shone out again to guide the Channel shipping safely past the most southerly tip of the Island.

Today the great light can be seen over eighteen miles away. On the clifftop, Walter de Godeton's lighthouse still stands as a reminder of his penance, and of the lives of those medieval monks, who, one after another, kept lonely vigil for two hundred years.

The Stronghold of Basing

WILLIAM PAULET, 1st Marquis of Winchester, rose to power in the reign of Henry VIII and managed his political career so skilfully throughout the turbulent Tudor period that he was still an advisor to the monarch, Queen Elizabeth I, when he died on March 10th, 1572.

At a time when most Tudor noblemen chose to forsake the castles of their ancestors and build more comfortable and modest homes, the Marquis decided to build a fortified house within the ruined boundaries of a Norman castle at Basing, which, in its turn, had been built upon the site of a Saxon stronghold. Permission to fortify a house now needed the King's consent for noblemen's castles were associated with private armies and the not long departed days when these had directly threatened the monarch. However. William Paulet was high in favour and he had no difficulty in persuading King Henry to agree to his request. The licence was granted in 1530.

The Marquis lived in fuedal grandeur in his great house which he filled with priceless treasures. Queen Elizabeth visited Basing in 1560 and was said to envy the magnificence of the house and gardens in which she was entertained with royal pomp and splendour.

The second marquis died four years after his father, in 1576, and the third, who was a poet, reigned at Basing until his death in 1598, so that it fell to the lot of the fourth marquis to entertain Elizabeth again in 1601, when her visit lasted for thirteen days. Honoured though he was to receive such a long visit from his queen the expense of entertaining Elizabeth, her entire court, and the numerous retainers, proved too much even for the wealth of a Winchester. He was forced to cut the high running costs of his household and decided to demolish a wing of the sprawling establishment. Even so, it remained one of the finest houses in England.

When his son, John, the fifth marquis, inherited the estates in 1629, they were still in debt and he lived quietly. By inclination he was a man of peace and a patron of the arts but, seeing the dangers which beset King Charles I, he looked to the defences of the house, for he was an ardent Royalist and was determined to hold Basing for the King if civil war should sweep the country.

The movements of the Marquis, a Roman Catholic, were carefully watched by the Parliamentarians for it did not suit them to have a papist stronghold in such a commanding place as Basing. On August 19th, 1641, a Mr. Sewer gave information to the House of Commons that he had seen a great many arms in the Marquis of Winchester's house at Basing and that the keeper of the armaments had told him that there were sufficient arms for fifteen hundred men. Consequently, on November 5th of that year it was ordered by Parliament that the Lord Marquis of Winchester should sell off his weapons to such tradesmen as would buy the same. The Marquis complied with the order and Basing House was left defenceless but for six muskets.

However, during the first months of the Civil War the Marquis gradually replenished his store of weapons and strengthened the already massive walls of his house, on every window of which he wrote "Aimez Loyauté". Many of Queen Henrietta Maria's friends sought refuge in the Roman Catholic household.

All the inhabitants prepared for the onslaught which they knew would come, for Basing was situated between London and the West country, and between the King's headquarters at

Oxford and the south of England, so that it was truly at the crossroads of an important theatre of war.

The Marchioness and her ladies made bullets from the lead torn from the roof of the house, and they were prepared to throw missiles from the towers on to any attackers below. They were under no delusions as to the bitterness of the warfare which would envelop them when it should come their way.

One hundred Royalist musketeers were sent from Oxford to help the defenders. They were led by Lieutenant-Colonel Peake and made a welcome addition to the local defence force. They arrived on July 31st – just in time – for the first of the long-awaited attacks was launched in August under the command of Colonel Norton. It had little effect on the strong fortifications, so more troops were brought up by a Colonel Harvey; but still the attacks failed.

The autumn mists turned to the fogs of November. Then early one morning the sound of horses' hooves and the beating of drums disturbed Basing. When the fog cleared the Marquis climbed the stairs to look out from one of the towers on the scene around the castle walls. Thirty-six guns were in position and seven thousand men surrounded Basing. They were commanded by the Parliamentary general, Sir William Waller. Three days of merciless pounding began but the garrison stood firm and returned the attack with such vigour that their opponents sustained heavy losses. The young Parliamentary soldiers, many of whom were from London, felt that they had no chance against those seemingly impregnable walls, and cried "Home, home". Finally, Waller withdrew to Farnham.

The defenders of Basing relaxed, but news from outside the garrison did not encourage them to expect speedy relief from their predicament.

The winter passed and severe privations were borne by the beleagured men and women of Basing. The spring of 1644 brought no comfort as they learned of the Royalists' defeat at Cheriton Down, near Alresford. Lord Hopton, the commander of the King's forces, arrived at the gates of Basing with wounded from the battlefield, whom he left behind in the care of his chaplain, Dr. Thomas Fuller, before passing on to Reading.

With the loss of this battle the course of the war in the south changed. The King was on the defensive and retired to his base at Oxford. Winchester and Basing were the only Royalist strongholds left in Hampshire.

The morale of the defenders was then further tested by rumours of treachery within the house. The Marquis learned with horror that his brother, Lord Edward Paulet, was conspiring with others to negotiate with Sir William Waller, as it was thought that the beleagured garrison must soon capitulate against such desperate odds. Lord Edward was denounced as a traitor. His life was spared but his punishment was severe. He was forced to act as hangman to his fellow conspirators. As he mounted the scaffold to execute the men whom he had persuaded to follow him, he surely felt that it was a terrible price to pay for the saving of his own life. Afterwards he was sent from Basing, and the name of Edward was never used by the family again.

During the summer the attacks were renewed. There were constant skirmishes around the walls. Supplies to the house were captured by the besiegers and, in turn, sorties were made by the defenders which inflicted losses on their opponents. The horses of the Parliamentarians were stabled in Basing Church. The lead coffins of the Paulet family were despoiled and the lead was used for the making of bullets, a strange twist of fate as they shot into the ancestral home.

By July 1644 the besiegers had pushed their trenches nearer the walls and were said to be "within half-musket shot", but a demand for surrender made by a Colonel Morley to "avoid the effusion of Christian blood" was rejected by the Marquis.

Sickness broke out in the garrison and food became scarce as the stores in the great barn, the fish in the ponds, and the nests in the dovecote became depleted. Another call for surrender came early in September and again it was refused.

At last relief came to the Marquis when Colonel Gage made a forced march from Oxford. He left the city at the head of four hundred men at 10 p.m. on September 9th and arrived at

Basing on the morning of September 11th having fought a way through enemy lines on Chinham Down. He collected supplies from Basingstoke and brought them to the stricken garrison. He then left one hundred men behind to help the defenders and returned to Oxford the following day via Pangbourne and Wallingford.

This brave action brought comfort to the defenders but they were hard pressed during September and October by the besiegers. Colonel Gage came to their help once more on November 4th. This time his journey was less hazardous as heavy rain had made the Parliamentarians seek safer winter quarters and their wet trenches had been vacated. Provisions were unloaded and the Colonel returned to Oxford, leaving the Marquis and his gallant band to face the rigours of the winter months.

Discontent and religious strife became manifest in the spring of 1645 and, on May Day, five hundred Protestants deserted and joined the opposing forces. The Roman Catholic Marquis was left with severely depleted numbers to face the summer months which brought sad tidings of Royalist defeats at Naseby and Bristol.

A heavy bombardment then took place under the leadership of the Dutch engineer, Dalbier, who tried to smoke out the Royalists by lighting piles of wet straw into which sulphur and arsenic had been poured. To encourage the besiegers, William Beech, their chaplain, preached a long sermon on Sunday, September 21st, on "More Sulphure for Basing".

Finally, on October 5th, the city of Winchester surrendered to Cromwell in order to escape capture by assault, and the General himself, with his New Model Army, then turned towards Basing to subdue this last Royalist outpost in Hampshire; a task which all previous commanders had failed to accomplish.

Cromwell took no chances. He climbed to the top of Winklebury Circle and surveyed the defences of the house he intended to take at all cost. Even in the face of this new threat the defenders remained defiant. They made a last sortie into the

village on October 13th and captured two prisoners, Colonel Hammond and Major King, who were riding to inspect the Parliamentary cavalry stationed on the opposite side of the house. Cromwell was furious and immediately sent a message to the house threatening dire consequences if any harm befell the prisoners. But they did not have long to wait for their release. Cromwell attacked Basing House at five o'clock on the morning of October 14th.

In spite of a defence aided by the setting of gunpowder traps, the throwing of hand grenades, and brilliant swordsmanship, the fate of Basing was sealed as Cromwell breached the walls by heavy bombardment. His numerous and well-disciplined troops swarmed through the gap to beat back the defenders.

The Marquis was taken prisoner. The famous architect, Inigo Jones, now seventy-two years of age, who had been in the house, was brought out wrapped in a blanket. All his clothes had been taken from him by the soldiers who were allowed to loot the house. Four priests were taken and were hanged. Other poor wretches perished in the underground cellars, where they had taken refuge, when the building caught fire in the turmoil which followed the capture of the stronghold.

Two days of determined destruction followed. Valuable treasure was lost for ever in the place which Cromwell's chaplain described as fit for an emperor's court, as he beheld its final glory before the invaders left it roofless and bare.

The Marquis was taken from his house and lodged at the Bell Inn in Basingstoke before being conducted to the Tower of London where the brave Marchioness was permitted to join him. Eventually, he was allowed to leave for France where he stayed until the Restoration in 1660. He was rewarded for his outstanding loyalty by the return of most of his lands, and he made his home at Englefield in Berkshire, which he had acquired by marriage. He died on March 5th, 1675, and is buried in the little church on the estate, in the peace of the countryside.

Basing House had been razed to the ground on Cromwell's orders. Permission was granted to all who wished to do so to carry away the stones and bricks, so that the once great fortress became the ruins one sees today. These were excavated at the beginning of this century by Lord Bolton, a member of the Paulet family, and recent work has revealed much more of the original foundations.

One delightful memento of the original house has survived Cromwell's holocaust intact. In the grounds is the sixteenth-century dovecote, still complete with its revolving ladder from which the five hundred nests could be reached. It stood throughout the siege and housed the birds which provided much-needed food for the beleagured men and women of Basing. Today it is a touching reminder of that once great house, the ruin of which is well worth a visit, for it bears poignant witness to the grandeur and bravery of its former occupants.

Dame
Alicia Lisle

THE battle of Sedgemoor was over. The Duke of Monmouth had been captured as he crouched in a ditch near Ringwood and his subsequent execution was a sad end to his hopes of becoming King of England.

Although his father, Charles II, had never acknowledged him as his legitimate heir, there were those who thought that the late King had married Monmouth's mother, Lucy Walter, therefore making the Duke his royal father's rightful successor.

Monmouth was persuaded that he had but to raise his standard in England, and proclaim his support for the Protestant cause, and men would flock to fight for him rather than have his unpopular and pro-Roman Catholic uncle, James II, on the throne.

The Duke sailed from Amsterdam in June 1685, and landed at Lyme Regis only to receive a scattered response to his call to arms as he marched through the West country. Those who did finally fight at his side were either killed or forced into hiding. Some found refuge in the New Forest, and two such fugitives brought disaster upon a Hampshire household.

Danger was not unknown to the owner of Moyle's Court, near Ellingham, for Dame Alicia Lisle had led an eventful life.

She was born at the Court in 1617, the daughter of Sir White and Lady Beconsawe. She grew into a high-spirited girl of some beauty, and married a young lawyer of her parents' choice when she was nineteen years of age. He was John Lisle whose father, Sir William Lisle, owned estates at Wootton in the Isle of Wight.

The young couple divided their time between their Hampshire and Island homes before settling in Winchester where John became recorder of the city and one of its two members of Parliament.

Although from a Royalist family, he sided with the Parliamentarians during the Civil War, and when Charles I was a prisoner on the Isle of Wight, John Lisle was one of the Parliamentary Commissioners who negotiated with the King at Newport in November 1648. In January of the following year he sat as a judge at the King's trial and was a signatory of the death warrant.

During the Commonwealth, John Lisle was appointed Master of the Hospital of St. Cross at Winchester in place of Dr. Lewis who was dismissed for his Royalist views. The fortunes of the Lisles seemed well established. Alicia had inherited Moyle's Court, John had the Wootton estates, and also bought the Manor of Chilbolton and a London home; but as they accrued their wealth they made many enemies, even among their Parliamentary friends, some of whom frowned upon the Lisle's aptitude for acquiring worldly possessions. The dispossessed Royalists positively hated them.

The restoration of the monarchy in 1660 spelled disaster for John Lisle. He was one of the Parliamentarians who was excluded from a pardon under the Act of Indemnity and Oblivion. He lost no time in leaving England and making his way to Switzerland, and Alicia was left to care for their large family alone. She was planning to visit her husband secretly at Lausanne in 1664 when the news was brought to her that he had been assassinated by English agents. His enemies had taken their revenge and she was left a widow with but slender means to provide for her children.

Although she was allowed to retain her own inheritance of Moyle's Court, the Wootton estates were granted to her Royalist brother-in-law, William Lisle. He was prepared to help her, but she quarrelled with him as she bitterly resented the fact that he was in possession of the property instead of her son, whom she regarded as the rightful heir.

Furthermore, she was desperately short of ready money. The small fortune which had been accumulated by her husband during the Commonwealth was confiscated, and by strange chance, King Charles II granted it to his brother, James, Duke of York. This brought the Lisle family to the notice of the Duke as most of the money proved difficult to trace, much to his annoyance. It was unfortunate in the light of later events as it emphasised that the determined lady and her affairs could be troublesome.

Troublesome to the Duke of York perhaps, but Alicia Lisle was also courageous in doing what she thought was her duty. She entertained nonconformists at her home, an act which was frowned upon by the authorities, especially after the Duke ascended the throne as James II. However, to her neighbours in the New Forest she was the well-loved mistress of the Court where her friends were always welcome. She was a devoted mother and contrived that her daughters made good marriages in spite of her straitened circumstances. Her family and friends looked upon her with love and respect and it was with overwhelming distress that they heard that she had been arrested for treason.

John Hicks, one time minister of a Unitarian chapel in Portsmouth and Richard Nel, a lawyer who was well known for his radical views, escaped the slaughter of Sedgemoor and made their way to Moyles Court, begging for shelter. It was a plea that the good-hearted woman could not refuse and she admitted them. But soon a squad of soldiers arrived to search the Court. They found the two men hiding and took them and their benefactress to Winchester, under arrest.

Dame Alicia was brought before Judge Jeffreys at the first of the assizes held in the west of England to try the unfortunate supporters of the Duke of Monmouth – the assizes which were to become known as the Bloody Assizes because of the brutality of the sentences passed by the notorious judge. Dame Alicia's trial was no exception. At first the jury were reluctant to find her guilty but the Judge so terrified the jurors that they gave way before his bullying and ranting and he obtained the verdict that he wanted. He then horrified the court by condemning her to be burned at the stake.

Before the court had recovered from its revulsion the second blow fell. The sentence was to be carried out that very afternoon. At that the men of Hampshire revolted. Some bravely refused to obey the order, others rioted in the streets. The Bishop and clergy of Winchester intervened and the sentence was postponed for five days.

Five days of agonising anxiety for Dame Alicia and her family followed whilst a plea for mercy was made to King James. He was adamant that the death sentence must stand – perhaps he remembered John Lisle's signature on his father's death warrant, and the elusive fortune of the late Parliamentary lawyer. However, the King did commute the sentence to execution by the axe, and so, on September 2nd, 1685, a venerable old lady of seventy years was beheaded in the square at Winchester.

Later, an Act of Parliament proclaimed that the verdict was invalid as it had been obtained by Judge Jeffreys through illegal practices. Alas, too late to help poor Dame Alicia Lisle who lies with her youngest daughter, Anne, in the peace of Ellingham churchyard – victim of one of the most infamous trials in English history.

The Earl's Cat

THIS is a story for cat lovers. It tells of the remarkable adventure of a cat which lived in Tudor times, when the lives of both men and cats were lightly valued, and it is therefore rather pleasant to know that at least one man and his cat enjoyed a high regard for each other.

The man, Henry Wriothesley, 3rd Earl of Southampton and Baron of Titchfield, was a patron of the arts. His friend William Shakespeare dedicated "Venus and Adonis", and "The Rape of Lucrece" to the noble benefactor.

Unfortunately, the Earl incurred the displeasure of Queen Elizabeth I by marrying one of her ladies in waiting, Elizabeth Vernon, without the Queen's consent. Later, he became involved in an intrigue against the Queen with his friend, Robert Devereux, 2nd Earl of Sussex, and both men were sent to the Tower of London and subsequently condemned to death. The sentence was later commuted to life imprisonment for the Hampshire earl but, even so, it was a dismal prospect for the young and active man of twenty-eight as he lived day by day, closely confined in that forbidding fortress.

Then one day the monotony was enlivened by a strange disturbance in the chimney, and after sounds of a slithering, slipping, bumping nature, soot fell into the empty hearth. This was quickly followed by a sooty, bedraggled bundle of fur from which peered two large frightened eyes. The Earl stepped over to investigate and stooped to touch his visitor. It leapt into his arms and started to purr loudly. He smiled as he soothed the ruffled but triumphant cat, and then paused in wonder for, as soot rubbed off on his hands, he realised that he was holding his

own black and white cat which he had left in his house in Holborn. Missing its beloved master, it had left its home to brave the noisy streets and dark alleys of Tudor London, and with that uncanny feline instinct which guides cats to their owners or past homes, had found its way to the Tower and to the chimney of its owner's cell.

The cat stayed to comfort the Earl as the lonely days passed into weeks and months; but happier times were to come for, with the death of the Queen and the accession of King James I in 1603, the Earl was pardoned and, with his cat, returned to the comfort of his London and Hampshire homes.

The King's favour restored the Earl to his rightful place at court and he quickly resumed his role of benefactor to the writers and artists of the day. His portrait was painted many times, but one which he regarded with particular favour showed him with his faithful, canny, feline friend.

Highwaymen

WELL-MOUNTED highwaymen in their many-caped coats, tricorne hats, with their faces half-obscured by black masks, have become legendary figures of romance and mystery. In reality they were often no more dashing in their appearance than modern 'muggers', and certainly they were just as strongly disliked by the law-abiding members of the community. The three highwaymen I am about to describe have little in common with the glamorous image that Dick Turpin and his black horse have acquired over the years. The first's attempt at highway robbery was a disaster.

It was on the evening of October 29th, 1785, that a Mr. Smith of Silchester was returning on foot from Reading market. Whether he had bought or sold at the market we do not know; probably it was both and he was on his homeward way with a reasonably full purse in spite of purchasing a few necessities, and some small gifts for his wife and family. It was not every week that a man trudged from Silchester to Reading at dawn and returned at dusk the same day, so the journey was worth a few mementoes.

The way was long and lonely and he was thankful that he had done the greater part as he passed over Burghfield Common and drew near to the Hampshire border.

Suddenly he heard the sound of horse's hooves behind him. His first thought was that here was a lucky man who had a horse to carry him home. The horseman drew nearer and steadied his pace. Perhaps he was a stranger to these parts and needed direction? Mr. Smith turned, eager to help for he knew the road well, and looked up into the face of a masked man. The stranger dismounted from his horse and moved threateningly towards the now frightened traveller saying that he would be a dead man if he did not hand over his money. Frightened he may have been but the man from Silchester was not going to hand over his hard-earned money so easily. He bravely attacked the robber. After a short scuffle the masked man fell to the ground. Smith siezed the bridle and mounted the man's horse. Before the highwayman had time to recover from his surprise his victim, and his horse, were well down the road – it was his turn to walk home.

The second highwayman of this tale had a more successful career but was markedly more improbable as a Gentleman of the Road. He was actually a gentleman of the cloth. The condition of his horse caused concern to his groom. The Reverend Darby's stableman would scratch his head in bewilderment for the horse was well groomed at night but in the morning he was tired and covered with foam. The man held his peace, it was not his place to enquire what his master did at night.

The mystery was solved when Parson Darby of Yateley was exposed as a highwayman who had not only committed sundry hold-ups in the neighbourhood, but had robbed the mail coach at Hartford Bridge on more than one occasion. His last haul was reputed to be in the region of five hundred pounds. The money was never recovered. It was thought that the Parson threw it into a pond as he was pursued after the robbery.

The exposure was a terrible shock to his parishioners who knew him as a kindly man who cared for the poor of his parish. Nevertheless he was duly hanged from a tree on what is now called Darby Green at Yateley.

What caused the Parson to take to highway robbery? Was it his slender stipend or, as some believed, heavy gambling debts? Perhaps he yearned for a more exciting life than that of a country parson – we shall never know for, unlike Thomas Boulter, he was not allowed time to write his memoirs before he was hanged.

There is no denying that Thomas Boulter was a robber and a

rogue, but, although he relieved many of their money, he never caused bodily harm to any man as he rode the length and breadth of England. His memoirs reveal him to be more of a confidence man than a pistol-toting desperado.

He was born in 1748 and, until the age of twenty-six, worked at his father's mill in Poulshot, Wiltshire. He was a striking figure, tall, fair-haired and pleasing in manner although born of parents who were both caught on the wrong side of the law at times.

Thomas became unsettled, life was too quiet, and the work at the mill too monotonous for the ambitious young man. In 1774 he decided to visit his sister at Newport in the Isle of Wight where she owned a successful milliner's establishment. He took his small investment out of the mill to enable him to open a grocer's shop in part of his sister's premises.

A year was long enough to convince Boulter that he was not meant to be a grocer, especially as he was losing instead of making money. His thoughts turned to other occupations. He craved excitement and he wanted money. A highwayman? The idea appealed to him and he began to lay his plans.

Boulter visited Portsmouth where he bought pistols, lead for slugs, and powder. Then he returned to Newport and thought he would try his hand at highway robbery on the Island. However, upon consideration, he realised that he could be easily trapped in such a confined area and decided to go to the mainland. He told his sister that it was time he visited their mother. As their father has just been transported for fourteen years for horse-stealing this seemed a reasonable explanation for his sudden departure for home, and he set off for Southampton where he called upon Mr. Cox, landlord of the Vine Inn, who hired out horses.

The day was fine as the would-be highwayman rode towards Salisbury. On reaching Millbrook he fancied a turn across Southampton Common, then made his way across country to the western road between Stockbridge and Sutton Scotney. As luck would have it, he met the Salisbury stage-coach carrying only two passengers. Here was an opportunity to begin his new career, but at the last minute his nerve failed him and he rode past. Then he thought that if he intended to become a high-wayman he really must make a start, so he turned his horse and rode back after the coach. He overtook the lumbering vehicle, drew alongside, and within a few minutes he had relieved both passengers of their money and their watches. He told them that he was in great need of money and it was only necessity that made him behave so badly. He then wished them a pleasant journey and took his leave. This apologetic attitude and politeness of manner remained with him throughout his nefarious career.

Alas, his first attempt had proved all too easy and profitable – Thomas Boulter was firmly set on the pathway of crime. He arrived at Poulshot with seven watches and forty pounds in his pockets.

The dutiful son saw his mother and then proceeded to make his way back to the Island. He stayed one night at Andover, where he rested at the Swan Inn. He robbed success-fully at Basingstoke and gained confidence. Before he reached Southampton Common he had robbed the occupants of a post-chaise, two country women as they returned from market after selling their wares, and two or three farmers. He rode into the port well satisfied, and boarded the packet for the Isle of Wight.

Boulder stayed with his sister for some time, relating the family news, and waiting for the hue and cry he had caused on the mainland to die down. While he waited he equipped himself with new pistols and new clothes. With money to spare he could afford clothes of good quality and gratify his wish to appear well groomed. He also wanted to acquire a first-class horse and he looked around for one to steal, but soon had the good sense to realise that it would be difficult to transport a stolen horse to the mainland without being apprehended. He crossed to Southampton alone.

On arrival, Boulter sought out his friend Mr. Cox and rode towards Lyndhurst on a hired nag. He joined company with an elderly gentleman as he left Lyndhurst to wend his way to Lymington. The two travellers chatted happily together as they rode along the next four miles, during which time Thomas unfolded an amazing tale of misfortune to his kindly companion. He said that he was a young tradesman who had fallen on hard times and, very reluctantly, it was necessary for him to ask for help from those he met on the road. The old gentleman shook his head – a sad story indeed. He opened his purse and counted out ten golden guineas, all he had with him. He gave them to the young man and said that he hoped his troubles would soon be over and that he would never have to resort to such a course again. The travellers parted company after the good man had been thanked most courteously by his wayward companion. Boulter was doing well, but he still needed a strong horse.

He made his way back to Totton, then decided to give up the search for that day and spent the night at an inn at Redbridge. He rose early, saddled his hired horse and spent a pleasant morning riding along the banks of the Test. He glanced down at the clear water from time to time. The trout darted under the grey stones and the long green weeds swirled in the depths as a kingfisher flew in the sunshine. What more could a man want? What indeed – but Thomas Boulter left the beauty of the river and turned back on to the highway. He managed to fit in a couple of robberies before he rode into Romsey where he stayed for an hour, and then crossed the New Forest to Fordingbridge. The Greyhound Inn provided him with refreshment but he still needed that horse. On to Ringwood, and this time luck was with him. He saw an excellent horse in a field and decided that it would carry him well but it was too light to chance taking it from its rightful owner. He waited until darkness fell, returned to the field, and led the horse through the night to Southampton Common where he left it to graze and proceeded to the Vine Inn to return his hired mount to Mr. Cox.

Boulter crossed to the Island, quickly settled his affairs and return to Southampton after buying a saddle and bridle. He caught his stolen horse and, carefree and confident, he journeyed into Wiltshire where he had more successful adventures before making his way to that ever-popular haunt of highwaymen – the London to Bath Road. He robbed at Maidenhead, Staines, and Windsor then quit the famous road, turned towards Wokingham, and rode over the Hampshire border to Hartley Row.

It had been a hard ride but he thought it safe now to draw rein at a roadside inn and take some refreshment. He bought a bottle of wine, drank half himself and poured the remainder over a slice of toast which he gave to his horse. Suitably refreshed, horse and rider made their way to Wiltshire, and Poulshot, where Boulter thought it wise to stay quietly with his mother for a few weeks.

Having implanted on the minds of the suspicious a picture of a devoted son caring for his mother's interest, Thomas Boulter set out once more to care for his own. He travelled through Devizes to Bristol, ever on the look out for suitable people to enrich his pockets, and always using that charm and courtesy which made his robberies more pleasant than most such highway encounters.

In the autumn of 1776 he returned to Hampshire to take up winter lodgings with a relative in a lonely part of the New Forest. Here Boulter lived in safe obscurity, but the relative was well aware of his occupation, and his restless nature, and took no chances. The lodger was only allowed out on foot so that he could not take a fancy to ride after adventure. Two months of such treatment was enough, and Boulter took leave of his host. His thoughts turned to the north of England – he saw before him a whole new territory to explore – and exploit – but first his wardrobe needed attention. He went to London and sought out a good tailor. When he rode to the north he wore clothes that any dandy might have envied.

In Newark, Leeds, and Doncaster travellers told tales of robberies by a gentleman of fashion. Later, in Manchester and Sheffield similar stories circulated, but at Ripon his luck ran out. A brave gentleman and his servant captured the highwayman and handed him over to the law.

It was Boulter's first setback. He was taken to York where, under the assumed name of Poore, he was tried and condemned to death, but on the very day set for his execution he was offered a reprieve. Naturally, there was a proviso – he must join His Majesty's army. Perhaps the judge thought that the life of such a fine upstanding man could be well used in the service of his country.

It was an opportunity for Boulter to make good – perhaps he thought so at first for he took up the offer and enlisted, but within a week he had deserted and was on his way to Nottingham.

With his customary charm and many apologies for having to ask such a favour, he persuaded a guard to take him up on a stage-coach and soon he was safely on his way to Bristol. On arrival, he walked by chance into the Ship Inn, became friendly with the landlord, James Caldwell, and found himself a partner in crime.

Boulter toured the West country, visited Leicester, and then returned to Bristol. Soon he was off again, this time to see his mother and to spend a brief holiday in Poulshot. Always the road called him back, and he continued to rob, sometimes alone, sometimes with Caldwell.

By this time high rewards were being offered for his capture, not only by the Crown, but by private individuals who had been robbed of their valuables. People were becoming a little tired of the well-dressed highwayman, despite his good looks and apologetic manner.

Once more Thomas Boulter was captured, this time in Birmingham, and once more he escaped death on the scaffold, on this occasion by cutting a hole through the wall of his prison cell. Off to Leicester he went, then south towards Dover, on another stolen horse. He now realised that sooner or later he would be taken if he stayed in England, and that at all costs he must make for the Continent. It was too late. The threat of war with France was very real and the ports had been closed.

So from Dover he turned and rode to Portsmouth – perhaps he could get to the Island and find refuge at his sister's house? It was no use, even the ferry was guarded. He grew desperate – Bristol – then down to Bridport – everywhere was closed. He went into an inn; a quick supper and then he would be on his way to the Isle of Portland where there would be no one to watch his movements in that lonely place. But even as he ate his supper he was being watched – the landlord recognised him as a wanted man and betrayed him.

Boulter was arrested. He was taken to Dorchester, then to London's dreaded prison, Newgate; but it was at Winchester that he stood his trial. James Caldwell was brought from Tothill Fields to join him – two rogues together, and it was inevitable that the death sentence should be passed on both, but even to the last Thomas Boulter exerted his tremendous charm. He begged for a respite of three weeks so that he could write the story of his career and inform the public of his misdeeds. The judge was so moved by his penitent manner that he granted the condemned man's request.

Did Boulter hope that he might escape again? If so, his luck had turned. He was hanged at noon on Wednesday, August 19th, 1778. The story of his career of crime, written in the condemned cell, has left us with a remarkable portrait of an eighteenth-century highwayman. A man whose ability, charm, and daring, should have found a better stage than the shadows of the King's highway and finally the gallows platform.

The Story of
Buckler's Hard

Buckler's Hard stands on the banks of the Beaulieu River near the ruins of the great Abbey which was founded by King John in 1205. The King granted the Abbot large tracts of disafforested land for farming purposes and, in addition, many rights and privileges including that of hunting in the New Forest; a privilege indeed, for the Norman Kings usually kept their hunting grounds for their own use. Abbotsstanding Wood is traditionally the place where the hides were erected so that the Abbots could aim carefully at the game which were driven towards them.

Change came to Beaulieu in the sixteenth century when King Henry VIII suppressed the monastic houses throughout England. On April 2nd, 1538, Abbot Stevens and twenty monks signed the deed of surrender in the chapterhouse of Beaulieu in the presence of the King's commissioners, and were rewarded with grants of pensions for their compliance with the King's orders.

The Abbey, its lands, and many of its privileges were sold the following August, for the sum of £1350 6s. 8d., to Thomas Wriothesley, 1st Earl of Southampton.

His descendant, John, 2nd Duke of Montagu, inherited the estates in 1709 at the age of twenty. He married Mary, the daughter of the great Duke of Marlborough, and was a man of distinction and great wealth. To add to his consequence, in 1722, King George I granted him the West Indian Islands of

St. Vincent and St. Lucia, together with their Governorship, and it was this bountiful gift that fired the Duke with the idea of developing Buckler's Hard into a thriving port, complete with a sugar refinery.

The Duke pictured his ships sailing into his own port (instead of those of London or Bristol), bringing valuable cargoes of sugar in their holds from his own islands.

It was a pleasant dream and seemed sure to materialise for it had much in its favour. One of the privileges inherited from the Abbots of Beaulieu was the right of free harbour and immunity from toll and wharfage in all ports throughout the King's Dominions. Another was the rare privilege of owning the bed of the River Beaulieu, a tidal river.

By 1724 the project was under way. The Duke gave a contract to Miles Troughton and William Edwards to demolish the old fulling mill house at Beaulieu and to remove all the materials to Buckler's Hard for the building of a warehouse. He also ordered that a quay should be built on the side of the river, but while all was going well at Beaulieu, the scheme was running into difficulties in the West Indies.

A deputy governor, Captain Uring, had been appointed, and he sailed for the Islands with seven ship-loads of settlers and their wives and families. Unfortunately, they received a very hostile welcome both from the native population and from the large number of Frenchmen who were already settled there. It was soon apparent that the Duke's scheme for introducing new settlers would not succeed, and after he had counted his losses, which amounted to around £40,000, he decided to forget his dream of a sugar port.

For twenty years Buckler's Hard remained dormant but early in the 1740s another scheme emerged. "Salisbury" a 48-gun ship had been built there in 1698, and this gave rise to a new venture. The Duke offered a shipyard on Beaulieu River for a very low rental, together with three loads of timber from his oak woods for every new house that was built. Timber was also at hand, of course, for the building of the boats, and in 1743 a James Wyatt from Burlesdon took up the Duke's offer. The new

project brought life to Buckler's Hard as men came to work and live in the growing community. In 1745, the *Surprise*, a 14-gun ship, was launched and two others were built before James Wyatt left the yard in 1748. John Darley took over the tenancy, and within six months a Henry Adams became the tenant of another yard. By 1750, Darley appears to have left, but William Marks, John Pewsey and Thomas Davies were all active.

51

However, it was Henry Adams who brought fame to Buckler's Hard.

Twelve merchant vessels and fifty-two men-of-war were built by Henry Adams and his sons. They included such ships as the *Illustrious* (the largest ship ever built in the yard), *Swiftsure*, *Agamemnon*, and *Euryalas*; all of which fought at Trafalgar in 1805.

The launching of a ship was the signal for a great gathering of people at Buckler's Hard. For many miles around the roads were thronged with carriages and waggons bringing sightseers to the banks of the river where scaffolding was erected, and booths set up, for their accommodation. Henry Adams had a large room built on to his house so that he could entertain the important guests under his roof.

The master shipbuilder died in 1805 at the age of ninety-two and left his two sons, Edward and Walter, to carry on the shipyard. All was well at first but after a few years of success they attempted too much. They undertook to build four new men-of-war at the same time. By 1818 they were in dire trouble as they could not finish the ships by the agreed date and were heavily fined for breach of contract.

The brothers disputed the fine and became involved in an expensive lawsuit with the Government. They lost the case and were unable to pay their heavy commitments – the business failed and the Adams' once flourishing yard was no more.

It was a sad day for Buckler's Hard, but over one hundred and twenty years later the river was filled with boats such as the Adams never knew, for special craft were fitted at Buckler's Hard in readiness for the Normandy landings in the Second World War.

Today, peace has returned to the river. The master's house is now an hotel, there are a few cottages, and a little chapel where once the children were taught at the Dame School – just a few reminders of the Duke of Montagu's dream town.

Hampshire Fairs

ST. GILES, WEYHILL, THE BOURNE REVELS – three fairs of Hampshire – not the only three, of course, for many towns and villages held fairs of some variety, but these three are representative of the types of fairs to which people went in bygone centuries to sell their wares, spend their money, enjoy the sports, or simply to gossip.

St. Giles of Winchester was rated the finest fair in England and amongst the greatest in Europe.

King William Rufus granted the fair to his kinsman, Bishop Walkelin, who completed the new Norman Cathedral, and demolished its predecessor, in 1093. The Cathedral needed money towards its upkeep and the grant of an annual fair in 1094 on the vigil, feast and morrow of St. Giles (August 31st to September 2nd) was most welcome.

In the reign of Henry II the period of the fair was extended to sixteen days, no doubt to the annoyance of the city's traders, for all normal business was suspended during fair time, not only in Winchester but for seven leagues (twenty-one miles) around the city.

On the eve of the fair the Bishop's representatives received the keys to the city from the Mayor and bailiffs. They rode from gate to gate around the walls and the keys were surrendered and the fair proclaimed. The procession then made for St. Giles' Hill where the Mayor and bailiffs were dismissed and the Bishop's own officers appointed for the duration of the fair.

Substantial tolls were levied by the Bishop on all traders who wished to sell their wares, a most profitable procedure as traders came to Winchester not only from distant parts of

England but also from Ireland and the Continent.

The stalls were set up in rows, or streets, which were named after the goods displayed for sale, or the nationalities of the vendors – thus, Silver Street or the Street of Caen. The monks of Winchester had their own stalls; they favoured drapery and spices – two commodities much in demand, for customers wanted stocks of good cloth and sewing materials to clothe their families and servants throughout the coming year; and the good housewife always needed spices to flavour and preserve the limited range of medieval food. English wool merchants were there to sell the finest wool in the then known world. Cloth merchants came from York, Leicester and Northampton. Lead and tin ingots were brought from the Cornish mines.

The jostling crowds thronged the streets, eager to find good bargains or to stare at the rich merchandise from across the sea. Silks, brocades, finely wrought metal work, brilliant gems, fine wines – all so exciting to those who knew little of the luxuries of life.

Then there were the jugglers, acrobats, wrestlers, and strolling players, the performing animals and pathetic freaks – all provided amusement when business was completed. People of strange complexions, those speaking strange languages, rich merchants, poor beggars – what a motley crowd – and what a hunting ground for pickpockets and thieves!

Provision was made, even for the light-fingered – if they were caught. The Court of Pieds Poudreux dealt quickly with the offenders before their "dusty feet" took them out of reach. Again it was the Bishop's bailiff who presided over the Court during the period of the Fair, and collected the fines. The city's normal dispensers of justice were not too pleased about that arrangement. But it was not only in the city itself that the fair caused an increase in crime. Bands of robbers waited along the highway to waylay the baggage trains of the merchants. Five mounted sergeants-at-arms were employed by the Bailiffs of the Fair to guard the pass of Alton, a densely wooded road between Alton and Farnham. It was essential to keep the roads free of bandits if the Fair was to prosper.

An even worse hazard than highway robbery struck the prosperity of the Fair in the fourteenth century when the Black Death swept across the land. It was a setback from which St. Giles' Fair found it difficult to recover for trade with the continent was disrupted for many years. Nearer home, in the fifteenth century, as the trade guilds grew in strength their members murmered louder about the suspension of trade in the city while the Fair was in progress. In 1451 there was a serious dispute between the Bishop and the Mayor which did not help matters.

Finally, King Henry VIII granted two fairs for the citizens of Winchester, one during the first week in Lent and the other on the day of King Edward the Confessor (October 13th) and the day following. This occurred at a time when the importance of Winchester, both commercially and constitutionally, was in decline, and also the more settled pattern of buying and selling goods was taking business away from the big trade fairs. The great days of St. Giles' Fair were over. Slowly the three fairs declined in power and size. These fairs continued until 1834 when it was decided by the Mayor and Corporation that they should be replaced by two new ones, one to be held in February for the sale of sheep and cattle, and one in October for pleasure. The latter was held in the High Street, until the ever-increasing traffic made it too hazardous and it was removed to the meadow at Bar End.

Weyhill Fair, though less important than that of St. Giles, could boast of a sale which, so far as is known, never took place in the cathedral city of Winchester. It is said that a man sold his wife at Weyhill, and that the incident gave Thomas Hardy the idea for his novel, *The Mayor of Casterbridge*!

The origin of Weyhill Fair is obscure. There is evidence that fairs were held on the windswept hill as early as the thirteenth century, but Weyhill stands at the crossroads of two ancient trading routes, one from Cornwall to the straits of Dover, along which Cornish tin was carried, the other from Holyhead to Christchurch Bay, where a settlement and port existed in the Iron Age, and was in use during the Roman occupation of

Britain. It seems possible, therefore, that traders exchanged their goods at Weyhill long before the fair was officially recorded.

The Mayor and Corporation of Andover held the rights of the Fair during medieval times, and occasionally tried to move the site nearer the town, but Weyhill always remained a large agricultural fair on the hill nearby.

Trading was so successful that three fairs were held during the year, on April 11th, the last Friday in July, and on October 9th. The last was the most important of all and continued for a week.

Before the fairs, shepherds could be seen bringing their flocks along the tracks to the hill, for sheep were the most important feature of the sales. It is said that as many as 100,000 were penned at one fair. Cheeses and hops were also in abundance. Hops were grown around Alton and Farnham, and growers from Surrey and Kent thought it worth while to bring their crops to Weyhill. Those from Farnham were considered to be of superb quality and in 1828 they fetched £7 per hundredweight compared with £5 for those grown in other areas.

The Farnham men travelled by way of Alton and joined up with growers from Bentley, Binstead, and Froyle. Although rivals in trade the growers were glad to meet on the road, exchange opinions and, no doubt, put the country to rights. Apart from anything else, there was safety in numbers, for highwaymen lingered on the roads and were on the watch for traders who carried large sums of money on their persons. Some businessmen took the precaution of hiding it down their top boots, or asking their wives to sew it into the linings of their waistcoats, but it was safer to be with good friends.

One year some travellers to the fair had an unexpected treat, in spite of having trespassed over private land. As they passed through Hurstbourne Priors they thought that a short cut through the park of the great house looked inviting. It was early, there was no one about, and they decided to take a chance. The men were embarrassed and a little apprehensive when they came face to face with the owner, Lord Portsmouth, who was returning from cub hunting. Fortunately for them his lordship was in a jovial mood and when they apologised for their behaviour he invited them all into his house for a good breakfast.

Fields were allocated for the livestock, and stalls for the produce, as at St. Giles. In fact, the stalls at Weyhill became permanent structures and were left up from year to year. In addition to the principal sales there was a medley of articles which tempted the less serious buyers to empty their purses on a day's outing to Weyhill. Clothes, sweetmeats, ale, of course, and an assortment of household goods, while from the village of Penton came the product of its local craft – shovels made for the granaries and malting houses. In the early nineteenth century when umbrellas were becoming more popular there were ample supplies at the fair. It was not only the ladies who bought them; the farm labourers were also good customers, for they found that the umbrellas, although objects of amusement only a few years before, provided good shelter as they plodded to work on rainy days.

Being a hiring fair, farm workers came to Weyhill if they needed to seek employment or if they were casual workers, for extra harvestmen were always needed by a prosperous farmer. If he was on the lookout for other workers he would see what token they displayed – wool for a shepherd, a piece of cowhair for a cowman, whipcord for the drover, or a tuft of horsehair for the carter. If agreement was reached the farmer would hand the man a shilling and both would know that a contract had been made for the next twelve months.

Some came to try their hand at the sports. As at most fairs, there was pony racing, cudgel playing, wrestling and prize-fighting, but perhaps the entertainment which the men enjoyed most of all was the ceremony which took place the night before the fair. To accommodate all who wished to participate, two "Horn Suppers" were held, one at the Star and the other at the Bell Inn.

Both hostelries kept a pair of ram's horns for the "Horning the Colt" ceremony. The horns were mounted in silver with a cup between them which held half a pint of ale – several times stronger than our present-day beers! Below was a grotesque head.

After dinner had been thoroughly enjoyed the landlord looked round the company to find any newcomers — or "colts". In vain a stranger might try to hide behind his neighbour, someone would be sure to know that he was new to the parish and the fair. "Are there any colts to be horned?" the landlord would enquire, and as a bashful newcomer stepped forward he would be grabbed and placed on a chair. An attendant would put the horns on his head and fill the cup with ale. Then he would sing:

"As fleet runs the hare, as cunning runs the fox,
Why should not this little calf grow to be an ox,
For to get his living 'midst briars and thorns
And to die like his daddy with a long pair of horns?"

All the company would join in the chorus:

"Horns, boys, horns: Horns, boys, horns!
Why shouldn't he ramble 'midst briars and thorns
And die like his daddy with a long pair of horns?"

The colt would then drink the ale, for which, by the way, he had to pay himself, and then he had to buy a further half-gallon to be shared between the company. After the ceremony the colt was duly admitted to the privileges of the parish and fair. One suspects that by the time the evening was over he and the other colts of that fair well deserved such honours.

The origin of the ceremony, of which slightly different versions are given, probably dates back to pagan times, but it continued until the end of the last century.

Our third fair, The Bourne Revels, was typical of many village fairs, for the day was predominately given over to pleasure, although some buying and selling was transacted at the fairground.

It was on the first Monday after July 12th that the people of the Bourne Valley went to the Summerhaugh, in the village of St. Mary Bourne, to enjoy themselves.

The very name of the field invited people to be happy – Summerhaugh, what a delightful name, derived it is thought from the Anglo-Saxon word *haga*, or hedge of hawthorn, which surrounded the field.

The river Bourne had to be crossed and, before the present bridge was built in the early nineteenth century, there was a simple wooden structure for the use of pedestrians only. A turnstile prevented any animals from using the rough bridge so that folk who were grand enough to come in carriages or waggons had to use the ford, likewise the horsemen, and the drovers who brought sheep and cattle for sale at the fair.

A stage for the sports was erected across the river, and the wrestlers and backsworders, or cudgel players, had to be prepared to take a ducking if they overstepped the platform, or "butt", though they cared little for that as long as they won a coveted prize and the admiration of the crowd watching from the bank. Although some bystanders might shrink from watching these sports there were always those who enjoyed seeing a man thrown, or cracked over the head with a cudgel, and if a competitor went into the river it was a cause for greater mirth.

The backsworders had their left arms tied to their sides so that they were unable to ward off the dangerous blows which came from an opponent's cudgel which was swung by the right hand. The umpire, or "umsher" as he was commonly known, called "Blood" or "Head" if a hit was scored, and the blood ran the required one inch, but it was "No head" or "Play on" if the claim was disallowed. Samuel Ayres, George Stacey, David Goodyear, and Maurice Pope were a few of the local men who played at St. Mary Bourne, but Thomas Black of Inkpen and Simon Stone of Somerset also came to the village. They were well known at many fairs and were considered to be notable exponents of the sport. For those who preferred less blood-thirsty games there were the yawning matches, which carried a prize of a fine cheddar cheese, or the jingling match in which eight or ten blindfolded men tried to catch the jingler as he darted about, ringing his bells. The man who seized him was awarded a purse of money, but if the jingler evaded his pursuers he took an award of cheese, a new hat, or a barrel of beer.

The cheapjacks were there with their tawdry goods, and, of course, the country people with their butter and cheese. The valley was noted for its malting trade and the ale tents were well patronised. Too well patronised by some, for there was evidence of drunkenness by the end of the day. This earned a censorious retort by William Allen who said of the Revels, "They are scenes of blood and drunkenness, sensuality and sin." Strong words, indeed, from one who had himself been a leading back-swordsman until, through a remarkable conversion by a wayside evangelist, he became a nonconformist minister.

Perhaps there were excesses to justify the minister's remarks, but for most people the revels provided harmless fun, and as they made their way home at eventide, many voted Bourne Revel Monday as the happiest day of the year.

The three fairs are but memories now, but in their time they catered for the needs of the populace, both in business and pleasure, and in these times of more sophisticated pastimes there comes the thought that perhaps our ancestors knew better how to enjoy themselves by providing their own amusements for their few leisure hours.

Colonel Boles
and the Defence
of Alton

ALTON was the scene of bitter fighting during the Civil War and the parish church bears the scars of battle to this day. There are bullets embedded in the south door, and the pillars are marked from the gunfire which shattered the sanctity of the church when Colonel Boles fought to hold the town for King Charles I against overwhelming odds.

It was in December 1643, that the commander of the King's western army, Lord Hopton, managed to outflank the Parliamentary forces stationed at Farnham under the command of Sir William Waller, who was heavily engaged in the siege of Basing House.

As Lord Hopton pressed on towards Sussex he left Lord Crawford to hold Alton with a troop of horse, assisted by Colonel Boles with a company of infantry. Hopton warned Lord Crawford to keep a watchful eye on the movements of Waller, a warning which seems to have been taken somewhat lightly as Crawford was pleased to exchange pleasantries with the Puritan commander when Waller was resting his men after sustaining heavy losses at Basing.

Lord Crawford ran short of wine and asked Waller if he could send him a butt of wine in exchange for a fat ox. The wine duly

arrived and Lord Crawford promised he would deliver the ox, but Waller replied that there was no need as he intended to come in person to fetch it. That night the Parliamentary commander kept his word and attacked suddenly. He marched his troops eastward as if Basing was his objective, then wheeled to the south and approached Alton from the west. Lord Craw-ford was nearly trapped. To prevent his lines of communication with Royalist Winchester from being completely cut he gave the order for the cavalry to retreat. On safe ground once more he galloped off towards Winchester to bring reinforcements to the town, leaving Colonel Boles and his infantry to hold out against Waller for as long as possible.

The Colonel and his men fought gallantly for several hours. The Puritans fired the thatched roofs of the houses and under cover of the smokescreen, advanced to the market place. The Royalists, hopelessly outnumbered, fell back, fighting as they went. They reached the churchyard, then sought shelter in the church itself. Colonel Boles ordered that the heavy oak door should be closed and told his remaining eighty men to be prepared to fight to the death.

The merciless attack continued, the door was battered down and bullets swept the church as the Parliamentarians swarmed into the building. Sixty Royalists fell, the remaining twenty faltered before the onslaught but their indomitable leader fought on – up the pulpit steps – striving to keep off his assailants. Six or seven fell before his flashing sword and then, at last, it was all over. The Colonel called the name of the King for whom he had given his all as a heavy blow from the butt of a musket crashed down on his head and he fell dead in the pulpit.

King Charles was grief-stricken when he heard of the fall of Alton and the death of the gallant Colonel. He said to his attendant, "Bring me a mourning scarf, I have lost one of the best commanders in the kingdom."

Colonel Boles was buried at Winchester Cathedral but, as a tribute to his heroic fight, a brass was erected in Alton Church and this bears the same wording as his memorial in Winchester:
"Alton will tell you of that famous fight,
Which ye man made and bade this world Good-Night.
His Vertuous life fear'd not Mortalyty –
His Body must, His Vertues cannot Die.
Because his Blood was there so Nobly spent
This is his Tombe; that Church his Monument."

Virgin's Crowns

THERE was a church in the manor of Abbotts Ann in Saxon days, but the present church of St. Mary the Virgin dates only from the early eighteenth century for it was completely rebuilt in 1716 by the Lord of the Manor, Thomas Pitt.

A colourful and controversial figure, Thomas Pitt, a Dorset man, made his way to India in his early twenties and started to trade, at first in opposition to the East India Company (which required courage) and later as one of its recognised agents.

As one might suppose this enterprising man made headway and became a Governor of Madras in 1698. He was interested in diamonds and was fortunate enough to buy one of outstanding quality in 1701 from a merchant named Jamchund. Nine years later he returned to England and acquired Abbotts Ann and other manors. He settled down to his responsibilities as an extensive landowner, became M.P. for Old Sarum, and also busied himself with the disposal of his magnificent diamond. At length he sold it to the Regent of France for the then huge sum of £135,000, and it remains with the state jewels of France today. "Diamond" Pitt, as he became known, was appointed a commissioner for the building of new churches and he tackled the work with his customary enthusiasm. Needless to say, his own manors were not neglected. With his vast fortune he could afford to restore or rebuild as he pleased. Abbotts Ann received special treatment at Pitt's own expense.

If some parishioners sighed as they watched their old church demolished at least they had the satisfaction of seeing, when the new church was completed, a medieval custom continued as the virgin's crowns were hung upon its walls.

Today this custom is still observed and a crown is awarded to any unmarried person of good character, whether man or woman, who has been born, baptised, and who dies within the parish.

The crowns, which are made of hazelwood, are decorated with white paper rosettes. Five paper gauntlets are attached to each crown to represent a challenge to any who may dispute the award.

On the day of the funeral the crown is attached to a wand which is carried in procession by two girls dressed in white. Afterwards, the crown is suspended from the gallery of the church for a period of three weeks so that all who enter must pass beneath it. If, at the end of that time, no one has challenged the worthiness of the deceased to receive the honour, the crown is taken down from the gallery and hung high on the wall of the church, together with the gauntlets and a scutcheon bearing the dates and name of the deceased.

It stays in position until it falls from the wall with age, but the crowns do not disintegrate quickly for the oldest one was dated 1740 when I visited the church recently. The newest crown was bright by comparison for it had hung only since 1973 when it was awarded to Lily Myra Annetts who died at the age of seventy-three.

One wonders how long this medieval custom will continue in the present change of pattern in village life, but it is encouraging to see that the parishioners themselves have designed the new church kneelers to highlight the ancient tradition.

Forty-nine beautifully embroidered kneelers commemorate by name those who have been awarded a virgin's crown, while other kneelers show Christian symbols or designs adapted from the stained glass windows of the church.

The hours of work devoted to the making of the kneelers under the direction of a Rector's wife, go to prove that even with the ever-increasing rush of twentieth-century life, people can still spare time to patiently work for the glory of God in a quiet corner of Hampshire.

Parish
Church Tales

THE church of Abbotts Ann is only one of many Hampshire churches with a special if not a unique feature, behind which lies a history. It may be a tombstone, a stained glass window, or even, as at Kingsclere, a weather vane. Whatever it is, its beauty and the story of its origin adds particular character to a place that was the focal point of the community in which its members, rich and poor, young and old, worshipped and shared their sorrows and their joys over the centuries. In this chapter a few of these churches are described.

At Soberton, in the sixteenth century, a butler and a serving-girl made a considerable contribution to the wellbeing of their church, for tradition tells that they paid for the building of the tower in 1525. Their sculptured heads look down from the western cornice and beside them are symbols of their trade, a key and a pail. In the centre is a skull, a medieval symbol that death is the great leveller, but it seems incredible that in life these humble people, employed at the old Manor House, managed to find the money to give such a beneficent gift. Still, miracles do happen and certainly the story inspired all the butlers of Hampshire and their fellow servants to donate the money for the restoration of the tower in 1880.

It was hardly beneficence that made King John give the tower of Kingsclere church its unusual weather vane, but King John was a law unto himself. At least St. Mary's Church there can boast that its weather vane is unique, for surely no other church has a bed-bug to turn in the prevailing wind.

A few may prefer to think of it as representing the patient tortoise of *Aesop's Fables*, but the majority accept the traditional story of King John's command that a bed-bug should be displayed on the church tower.

It was King Henry II who built a small castle and a hunting lodge on Cottington's Hill near Kingsclere so that he could enjoy his favourite sport in Freemantle and Pamber forests, and it was there that King John was staying, around the year 1205, when he was caught in a dense fog on his return from a day's hunting.

The King rode into the village and decided that he would stay the night at the local inn rather than continue further south to reach the lodge.

Unfortunately, the landlord had not been able to prepare for his royal visitor. John spent a most uncomfortable night and was badly bitten by bed-bugs. His well-known anger was roused, perhaps justifiably on this occasion, and he ordered that a likeness of the troublesome creatures should adorn the tower of the parish church for ever.

A contemporary of King John's chose to adorn the Church of St. James at Bramley in a rather more skilful and seemly manner. He painted the wall of the church to tell the story of the murder of Thomas à Becket, which took place during vespers at Canterbury Cathedral in the year 1170. The unknown artist executed his work within fifty years of the killing, and painted it with a concern for detail not always observed by others, for whereas the Archbishop is sometime shown in eucharistic robes, at Bramley he is correctly dressed for vespers in his habit.

A fifteenth-century artist who also came to Bramley followed his predecessor's example for he, too, paid attention to detail when he painted St. Christopher carrying the Christ-child across the river. He included a hermit to hold the lantern, a fisherman, two mermaids each holding a looking glass and a comb, and, in the background, the sea with ships rocking on the waves. What a joy that picture must have been as the villagers entered the church, for few, if any, would have seen the sea or ships, or known of mermaids. They may have known about St. Christopher and his act of service to his Lord, but the artist wanted to teach them more and make the story very real to them.

An older example of medieval craftsmanship can be seen in All Hallows, the parish church of Whitchurch, for here lies a tombstone on which is carved a figure of Christ. His right hand is raised in blessing and the left hand holds a book. There is also a simple Latin inscription which, translated, reads: "Here buried rests in peace the body of Frithburga." The stone is dated by experts as being between 800 and 900 A.D. but nothing is known about Frithburga. It is thought that she was a lady of noble birth; probably she was connected with Wherwell Abbey, but her tombstone keeps it secret. It was found embedded in the wall of the church when restoration work was carried out in 1868.

Another stone, reputed to be 50,000 years old, is the Sarsen stone which lies beneath the parish church of Eversley where the Reverend Charles Kingsley was Vicar in Victorian times. He walked unknowingly over it for it was not discovered until 1940.

The Reverend Charles Kingsley with his strong views on Roman Catholicism would not have been happy as the incumbent of Tichborne Church, for there the north aisle is used as a Roman Catholic chapel by permission of James I who granted this most unusual favour to his loyal subject, Sir Benjamin Tichborne.

The chapel holds the family's monuments, one of which attracts immediate attention. It is the statue of a blue-eyed boy clothed in a brilliant red robe. It bears the date 1619 when the boy, Richard, son of Sir Richard Tichborne, died under tragic circumstances.

The story is told that a gypsy went to the door of Tichborne House and asked for food. She was refused, and as she turned away she laid a curse on the unfortunate child. She said that he would die from drowning and even foretold the day on which the tragedy would occur. One would have thought that having been forewarned the disaster could have been averted. Certainly precautions were taken, for servants took the child on to Gander Down, well away from the River Itchen which was seen as a possible source of danger. But the attendants must have been lulled into a sense of false security by their vantage point on high ground, and were careless of their charge. The child fell into a very deep cart-rut which was full of water and he drowned. The gypsy had taken her revenge.

If few parish churches can show an aisle which is used by members of a different denomination some still have a squire's or lord of the manor's pew, but it is rare to find one so well endowed as Minstead Church in the New Forest, which has no less than three Georgian "Parlour Pews".

The church organ is now housed in the Minstead Lodge Pew, but the Castle Malwood Pew, and the Minstead Manor Pew, still retain their fireplaces and chimneys, and their outside entrances, together with their comfortable furnishings.

How envious the children from the charity school must have felt as they walked sedately up the stairs to the Plain Top Gallery, which was built in 1818 to provide free seats for them and the poor of the parish. It eventually became known as the Gypsies' Gallery, as the nomads of the forest came into the church and made for the place where there was no pew rent to worry them. The pews down below were reserved for those who could pay the rents for them. Let us hope that the fires in the "parlour pews" were stoked well enough by the families' retainers to shed a warm glow over the whole congregation – not forgetting the parson and the clerk who occupied the three-decker pulpit.

The Church of St. Mary, Selborne, is remarkable for the superb memorial window to its famous eighteenth-century curate, Gilbert White. It shows St. Francis preaching to the birds, and ninety varieties are included in the window – every kind mentioned in the great naturalist's book, *Natural History and Antiquities of Selborne* which was published in 1789. It is a beautiful window and was placed in the church in 1920 to give pleasure for many years to come.

Another twentieth-century gift beautifies Romsey Abbey, the parish church of that lovely town on the River Test. It is a magnificent curtain embroidered with figures of saints, and on the tympanum above there is the figure of Christ in Glory, with two angels. Byzantine in style, its vivid colours stand out against the sombre background of the ancient abbey. It was embroidered by members of the Southampton College of Art in 1961 under the direction of its designer, Mrs. Maureen Helsdon. It is surely a happy thought that this beautiful work of art, which will pass into the history of the abbey, has been created by Hampshire people with the same love for a parish church in the twentieth century as were so many fine gifts of earlier times.

Brusher Mills – Snake Catcher

MANY huntsmen have passed stealthily through the glades of the New Forest – many have drifted into the mists of time, but Harry Mills is still remembered for the strange quarry he hunted – snakes.

Strange? Yes, but old countrymen knew old remedies. An adder bite was treated by an ointment made from the adder itself and, before medical aid was readily available, the country folk ran quickly to a snake catcher if man or beast was bitten by a venomous snake.

Harry Mills had no fear of adders. He handled them with his bare hands, immunised from their deadly sting, some said, by the amount of rum he drank.

Be that as it may, he caught his prey and popped them into an old tin. No doubt he then took his pick to make the precious ointment. The surplus snakes he sent to the London Zoo to provide delectable morsels for the secretary birds and other creatures who enjoyed New Forest snakes as part of their diet.

Harry Mills took time off from this strange occupation whenever a cricket match was played at Balmer Lawn. He became a familiar figure as he carefully swept the pitch between innings, and so acquired his nickname, "Brusher" Mills.

He was born at Lyndhurst and was nearly forty years of age when he left the town to live in the solitude of the forest. He settled in the woodlands near Brockenhurst, that delightful village where forest ponies wander at will and stop to drink from the stream that meanders across the main street.

Brusher chose a stout holly tree around which to build his mud hut, knowing that the shiny evergreen leaves would provide a waterproof shelter for his primitive dwelling. This was his home for nigh on thirty years by which time an old forest law entitled him to claim the land on which it stood. So, he decided to build a more spacious hut to give him greater comfort in his old age. But just as it was nearing completion the vandals struck. They tore apart his new home and it was a sorry sight which greeted Busher Mills when he returned from his work in the forest. He gazed at the destruction before him and his heart and his spirit were broken. All he had asked of life was to be left in peace in the silence of the woodlands. He never recovered from the shock of seeing his new house in ruins.

He died soon afterwards and his friends buried him in the quiet churchyard of St. Nicholas, Brockenhurst, said to be the most ancient church in the New Forest.

The gravestone bears a carving of the old man at the door of his hut; in one hand he grasps a staff, in the other – snakes. The inscription tells his story:

"This stone marks the grave of
Harry Mills
(better known as Brusher Mills)
who for a long number of years
followed the occupation of
Snake catcher, in the New Forest.
His pursuit and the primitive way
in which he lived caused him to be
a subject of interest to many.
He died suddenly July 1st, 1905
aged 67 years."

The
Royal Escape
To France

COLONEL GEORGE GOUNTER rode towards his brother-in-law's house in the sleepy village of Hambledon on October 13th, 1651. The lanes were carpeted with gold as the leaves fluttered down in the slight breeze, and the sun's rays caught the bright berries which still clung to the hedgerows, but the Colonel did not notice the beauty which surrounded him for his mind was troubled. Gounter was well known for his Royalist sympathies. He had served King Charles I in the Civil War, and in the years of the Commonwealth his movements were watched with suspicion by his Puritan neighbours. Recently his travel had been restricted to within five miles of his home at Racton and it was only on the payment of a substantial fine that he had regained greater freedom of movement. Yet, here he was, riding dangerously on the King's business, for Charles II had made an abortive attempt to claim the throne and was now a fugitive after the disastrous battle of Worcester.

So far, Charles had evaded capture by the Parliamentarians through the help of loyal subjects who were ready to risk death itself to protect their King. He had been passed from one hiding-place to another, including the famous oak tree at Boscobel, whilst attempts were made to find a vessel to carry him to France, the only way his safety could be ensured; for, if captured, it was more than likely that he would suffer the same fate as his father. Colonel Gounter knew full well that he would face death himself if the hastily laid plans for the King's escape went awry, but he rode steadfastly towards the manor house where his sister, Ursula Symonds, ran to greet him for she had seen his approach from a window. She was delighted at his coming and wanted to know if he had really managed to pay the fine as she knew that he had been hard pressed to raise the necessary money. He assured her that all was well, and answered her enquiries about his wife and children before asking if her husband, Thomas Symonds, was at home.

The Colonel was disappointed to hear that Thomas was in Portsmouth and that it was unlikely that he would return before the evening. He explained that he had called to borrow a pair of greyhounds as he, their cousin Captain Thomas Gounter, and a friend, had a mind to enjoy an afternoon's coursing on Broad Halfpenny Down. Ursula said that he might have the dogs and welcome but she was downcast that his visit was to be so short. She suggested that the sportsmen should return for supper, and if they so desired, stay the night in her somewhat small but comfortable home.

Colonel Gounter said that the party would be larger than she thought. The friend, a Mr. Barlow from Devon, would be accompanied by his servant, and later they were to be joined by two other men, Colonel Phelips and William Jackson, a young countryman.

Mistress Symonds replied that all were welcome under her roof. She little realised how relieved her brother felt when he heard those words, for it was an invitation which he had hoped to receive, and it meant far more to him than his sister could know at the time.

After collecting the greyhounds, the Colonel rode off to rejoin his cousin and Mr. Barlow, who were waiting for him on the downs. No doubt their exercise looked natural enough to any traveller who crossed the downs that afternoon, but their hearts were not in their sport. The day continued fine and the going exciting, but Mr. Barlow in particular was tense and anxious. He watched the shadows lengthen on that late autumn day and was thankful when at last Colonel Gounter turned his horse towards Warnford to meet the other members of the party, leaving him and Captain Thomas Gounter to continue their sport.

George Gounter rode into Warnford and saw two horsemen approaching along the main street. He looked at Colonel Phelips and then at the dark young man who rode by his side. No sign of recognition passed between them. Gounter rode on until he saw an ale house. He dismounted and called for refreshment. He evoked little interest as he slowly drank his beer, paid his reckoning, remounted and turned his horse towards Warnford once again. He appeared to be in no hurry as he rode through the town, but once he was clear of the cottages, he put his horse to a gallop and rode hard after the other two horsemen. He found them waiting for him under the shelter of some trees and slowing down his horse, he drew rein and dismounted. William Jackson held out his hand and Colonel Gounter bent to kiss it – "Your Majesty" he said softly, then raised his eyes to look upon King Charles II, the most hunted man in England.

After exchanging a few words the horsemen pressed forward towards Hambledon, and presently Gounter turned aside to summon Mr. Barlow to the King's presence, for the "gentleman from Devon" was none other than Lord Wilmot, the King's most faithful courtier, who needed no bidding but rode swiftly to the King.

Captain Thomas Gounter, and Robert Swan, Lord Wilmot's servant, joined the party, then rode ahead down the hill to make sure that the way was clear. The greyhounds ran behind them little knowing that they, too, were playing a part in the making of history. The King, Lord Wilmot, and the two Colonels, followed, but the journey was uneventful and the little cavalcade entered the grounds of Thomas Symonds' house.

The party was warmly welcomed by Ursula Symonds who regretted that her husband had not yet returned, but she led them to a comfortable room and brought them wine. She was somewhat discomposed as she watched Will Jackson, in his rough country clothes, at ease in his chair while his elders and betters passed round the refreshment. When the glasses needed replenishing she hinted broadly that he might lend a hand and he jumped to his feet and busied himself, to the embarrassment of his companions. Charles regarded Lord Wilmot with amusement as he knew that most correct gentleman was acutely distressed at having to accept such service from his King. Mistress Symonds suggested that they should wait no longer for her husband as he might have been delayed by business in Portsmouth, and her guests followed her to the dining room where the table was laid with a more than ample repast. The meal was hardly under way when the outer door was heard to slam and soon their host entered the room.

It was quite obvious that it was not business that had detained him but rather that he had spent a most convivial day with some friends. He swayed slightly as he surveyed the company and remarked that a man could not leave his house for a day but that it was filled with strangers on his return. However, when he realised that it was his brother-in-law and his companions who sat at his table he readily echoed his wife's warm welcome. He then walked round to inspect his guests more closely. He came to the King in his countryman's disguise. The shorn hair and plain clothes puzzled Thomas Symonds. Suddenly he looked reproachfully at George Gounter and exclaimed, "Here is a Roundhead, I never knew you keep Roundheads' company before." There was a moment's pause, then the Colonel collected his wits and assured his host that the young man was his friend and would do the Royalist household no harm. Thomas Symonds was satisfied. He clasped the King's hand and said, "Brother Roundhead, for his sake you are welcome." The tension passed and throughout the remainder of the supper it pleased the tipsy host to pretend that he was a Roundhead himself, much to the mortification of his poor wife who was already ashamed of her drunken husband.

His puritanical pose did not deter Symonds from drinking freely, and as he pressed more wine upon his guests he seemed to have the particular intent to make the young Roundhead as inebriated as himself. Lord Wilmot and Colonel Gounter grew uneasy but the King thoroughly enjoyed himself, and with his quick wit parried the thrusts from his host's tongue about his roguish Roundhead views. At the same time the young man knew that he must keep a clear head if he was to overcome the dangers that might await him the next day, and when Symonds' attention was diverted he passed more than one glass of wine to his neighbours at the table.

The hour grew late and still the host detained his guests, until his brother-in-law whispered to him that if they could persuade the young Roundhead to go to bed the older men could really be merry. Symonds saw the sense of this proposal, and thankfully George Gounter showed the King and Colonel Phelips to their bedchamber; while Lord Wilmot and Thomas Gounter kept their host in good humour as he wanted to rise from the table and accompany his Roundhead friend.

The next morning, presumably with some heads clearer than others, the household rose early and the guests were soon cantering away from the gates of the manor. On the downs the party divided and the King and Lord Wilmot, with Colonel Gounter as their guide, rode towards the coast. That evening, after much bargaining, a Captain Tattersall agreed to take the King and his courtier to France, and the following morning George Gounter stood on the beach at Shoreham and watched the *Surprise* sail slowly away on the tide. The Colonel turned for home, his mission was safely accomplished, and he had been assured by the King that none of those who had helped in the escape should be named until the day he could come to claim his rightful throne.

Nine long years were to pass before that day dawned and the King returned to England, but he did not forget those who had befriended him. A bowl was sent to Thomas Symonds and his good lady to remind them of the night on which they entertained a "Roundhead" at their supper table.

William Gilpin
of Boldre

THE parish church of Boldre, dedicated to St. John the Baptist, is set amongst the trees of the New Forest, the very essence of peace and beauty. By the side of the churchyard gate there is a stile, to recall the days when there were no cattle grids to prevent the forest ponies from wandering into the churchyard, and so the gates were often padlocked. It seems that the serenity of such a place could never be disturbed, but when the Reverend William Gilpin was inducted as Vicar in 1771 he nearly despaired as he felt that his new parish was beset by dishonest dealings, and that most of his parishioners were little better than vagabonds.

The children were quite uneducated, even by the standards of those days, and were clothed in little better than rags. Their parents were poor and turned to poaching and smuggling as a normal way of life. There was venison and game to be had in those forest glades, if one dared risk the severe penalties for taking them, and, being near Lymington and the coast, illicit cargoes could be collected and passed through the forest along the secret route known as the "Smugglers' Way". As told in the chapter on smugglers' tales, the table tombs of Boldre made excellent hiding-places for kegs of brandy, until a team of pack-horses could be brought to carry them further inshore to Burley and Ringwood, where those who had no qualms about buying duty-free merchandise were waiting to receive the illegal consignment.

William Gilpin was a man of great resolution. He had been headmaster of a school in Cheam for many years before moving to Boldre, the living of which had been presented to him by one of his former pupils, William Mitford. Gilpin had conducted his school on progressive lines unknown in the educational systems of the eighteenth century, and had inspired his boys not only to learn and play well, but to become self-reliant and, also, to care for those less fortunate in life than themselves. Mr. Mitford must surely have known that he had placed the wayward parish in the hands of the right Vicar.

William Gilpin set to work to educate the children of Boldre – the "three Rs" for the boys, together with a suitable trade; reading and sewing for the girls, and, no doubt, instruction in the Catechism for both sexes. He provided the children with warm clothing and, in addition to his good work for the younger generation, he opened a poorhouse for the benefit of his older parishioners.

The Vicar financed a considerable number of charitable schemes by writing and illustrating books about his travels around England, which he had undertaken during the school holidays at Cheam. These books made William Gilpin's name widely known throughout Britain. Many of his readers learned of the beauties of their native land for the first time by reading his detailed descriptions, and studying his clear illustrations of the many places which he had visited.

Among the books he wrote were *The Wye and South Wales, The Lakes, Forest Scenery, The West of England and the Isle of Wight,* and *The Highlands.* Few people were able to enjoy extensive holiday tours through Britain in those days, and of those who were fortunate enough to do so, none had described their travels as vividly as William Gilpin. His books were popular and his profits enriched his charities.

In spite of the time he devoted to the poor, to his writing, and to making the vicarage garden into a place of beauty, the Vicar was increasingly concerned with the moral welfare of all his parishioners. On one famous occasion he looked askance on the affairs of a rich farmer, who enjoyed the company of the

opposite sex too much. He admonished the errant farmer very strongly. This had little effect and so William Gilpin decided that stronger measures were necessary. Under the threat of excommunication, he made the farmer and his latest mistress stand in the church clad in white penitential robes, much to the gratification of the congregation.

As the years passed by, the earstwhile rogues of Boldre grew to love their Vicar, and when he died in 1804 they erected a monument to his memory in the north aisle of the church, extolling his many virtues and their gratitude for his care of them during his long period of office – over three decades.

In the churchyard there is an inscription on his tomb and that of his wife Margaret, saying that in a happier land "it will be a new joy to meet several of their good neighbours who now lie scattered in these sacred precincts around them", a joy richly deserved by the good Vicar and the wife who shared in his charitable life.

The Rufus Stone

In the heart of the New Forest, between Stoney Cross and Cadnam, stands the Rufus Stone, marking the place where a tyrant King was struck down by an arrow nearly nine hundred years ago. By whose hand that arrow was sped from the bow is a secret which the forest has kept throughout the centuries.

William the Conqueror, Duke of Normandy, bequeathed his English kingdom to his second son, William Rufus, rather than to his first-born, Robert, as he feared that his weaker, elder son would be unable to rule the newly-conquered, still turbulent land.

William Rufus reigned for thirteen years after his father's death, and made himself the most hated man in the kingdom. His disregard for the laws of God and man made many long for his death, but few could have thought that it was so near when he rode out to hunt on that fateful day in August 1100.

Sir Walter Tyrrel, son of the Lord of Poix in Picardy, was one of the hunting party, and to him was attached the blame for shooting the arrow which missed the running stag, hit an oak tree and glanced off to pierce the King to the heart. Tyrrel did not stay to argue. He fled from the forest in the confusion, and made towards a village where he could ford the Avon, a village which today bears his name, Avon Tyrrel. Tradition tells that he stopped at the backsmith's forge to have the shoes on his horse's hooves reversed in order to confuse his pursuers. He managed to outstrip them and arrived at Poole harbour where he embarked for France and safety. It is probable that he carried the news of the King's untimely demise to Robert, Duke of Normandy, who, not unnaturally, considered himself to be the rightful heir to the English kingdom.

Back in the New Forest the King's body was abandoned by his followers who, like Walter Tyrrel, fled from the scene with utmost speed. His younger brother Henry had no thought in mind but to reach Winchester as quickly as possible. Here he had himself proclaimed King before anyone could forward the claim of the absent Robert.

It was left to a charcoal burner, by the name of Purkis, to find the body and place it on his rough cart. He took it to Winchester and there the King was buried, swiftly and unmourned, beneath the tower of the Cathedral.

In due course Robert came from Normandy to claim his English throne. His army confronted that of his brother Henry at Alton, but, true to his father's opinion of his weak character, Robert gave way to his younger brother, accepted his terms, and returned home, leaving Henry I as undisputed King of England.

On his deathbed Walter Tyrrel vowed that he had not killed William Rufus. Who had? Was it by accident, or had a murder been planned by those who had good reason for wanting Rufus off the throne? These are questions which have remained unanswered. The oak off which the arrow glanced was said by Lord Delaware to be standing in 1745. He rightly assumed that it would not stand much longer as it had already overreached its natural life-span, and he erected the now famous stone to commemorate the place where the King died in Canterton Glen.

The
Tichborne Dole

Hɪsᴛᴏʀʏ will record that the twentieth century saw the installation of women in high positions throughout the world, positions which in both eastern and western countries were once thought to be the prerogatives of men, but only time will tell if these outstanding women are remembered with as much gratitude seven centuries hence as is the Lady Mabella Tichborne who lived in the thirteenth century. She did not seek fame but through a brave act, performed for the benefit of others, she has her place in the history of Hampshire, and is remembered beyond county boundaries when any speak of ancient charities.

It is uncertain when the Tichbornes first lived in the small village of that name, which is situated near Alresford. According to one member of the family, Chidiock Tichborne, they were there two centuries before the Norman Conquest, but this seems doubtful. However, he must be forgiven if he did exaggerate and boast too proudly of his ancestral line for the unfortunate man was about to be executed for his part in the Babington Plot, whereby the Roman Catholics hoped to place Mary, Queen of Scots on the throne of England.

There is documentary evidence that the Bishop of Winchester, Henry de Blois, granted part of his Tichborne estate to form a new manor for Walter de Tichborne in, or shortly before, 1135, and it is likely that he created the adjoining parish of Cheriton about the same time. Also, it is known that a house was in existence by the thirteenth century for the Tichbornes were given permission to hold divine services there in 1293.

It seems, therefore, that the family was well installed in the village, and had received the honour of a knighthood, when Sir Roger Tichborne granted his wife's request for a charity to be established for the poor of the parish.

It was the way in which it was granted that has lent colour to the thirteenth-century story of the Tichborne Dole.

The Lady Mabella was on her deathbed when she asked her husband if he would give her the means to leave a dole of bread to any poor parishioners who should come to the door of Tichborne House on Lady Day (March 25th).

Sir Roger must have been an extraordinarily cruel man for he vowed that he would give for the purpose of the charity, the corn from land around which his wife could circulate while a torch burned. As he looked down on the pathetic Lady Mabella he must have thought that he would never be committed to give anything at all to the poor on behalf of his dying wife. But she rose from her bed and, being too weak to walk, she crawled round the field.

Ill as she was, Lady Mabella managed to encircle twenty-three acres before the torch failed. She was carried, exhausted, to her bed. Perhaps the cruelty of her husband made her think that some future Tichborne might scoff at the vow, so, before she died, she made sure that none should forget the charity for which she had paid with her terrible ordeal.

She laid a solemn curse on any Tichborne who might think fit to neglect the distribution of the bread. Her muttered curse foretold that a generation of seven daughters would be born, the family name would die out, and the house would fall down if the vow was broken.

Throughout the centuries the bread was faithfully distributed. During the Tudor period the house was largely rebuilt, and this house forms the background to a picture painted by the Flemish artist Giles Tilburg to show Sir Henry Tichborne distributing the Tichborne Dole in 1670, surrounded by his wife and family, their friends and retainers, and the villagers to whom the loaves were given.

But towards the end of the eighteenth century it was considered that many called to receive the Dole who were not entitled to it. Rogues and vagabonds were accused of joining the legitimate beneficiaries, and the ceremony was not appreciated by the local magistrates. In 1796 the Dole was discontinued and a sum of money was distributed to the parochial poor in place of the bread. Many local people thought of the curse, and waited to see what would happen. They were not disappointed.

In 1803 part of the original house fell down. It could be argued by the sceptical that it was a mere coincidence, especially as the house was again being rebuilt, but more was to follow. Sir Henry Tichborne who succeeded to the baronetcy in 1821 was the father of seven daughters but no sons.

It was therefore thought expedient to revive the Tichborne Dole, and it continues to this day. All the parishioners of Tichborne and Cheriton now receive flour – a gallon for every adult and half a gallon for every child, when they assemble at Tichborne House on Lady Day.

The field around which Lady Mabella made her remarkable progress is situated by the road which leads from Cheriton to Alresford, and it is still known as "The Crawls".

Queen Anne is Dead

Many travellers have journeyed towards London to find fame and fortune, but in 1714 a young Londoner by the name of John Carter reversed the procedure and left the capital to seek his fortune in Portsmouth.

As Carter left his home he heard the sound of tolling bells and learnt that Queen Anne had died. The country's future seemed uncertain, as plot and counterplot had revolved round the dying Queen, who had produced no living heir to the throne.

George, Elector of Hanover, had been declared her rightful successor, and was strongly supported by the Whig government, but the Jacobites still hoped that they could make James Stuart, the Queen's half-brother, King of England.

Carter cared little for affairs of state and strode resolutely along the Portsmouth road for he had a journey of seventy miles before him. A few days later, tired and dusty, he reached the city and was challenged by the sentry on Ports Bridge. The young man told him of his long journey from London and spoke of the Queen's death, no doubt feeling rather proud that he was the first to bring such an important piece of information to the great port, but his pride was soon shattered.

The impressive news was quickly conveyed to the Governor, Sir John Gibson, outwardly loyal, but thought by many to have Jacobite leanings. Perhaps because of his own misgivings, Sir John immediately accused John Carter of spreading seditious rumours and had him clapped into prison – a fine beginning to his brave new life!

By good fortune the official messenger arrived almost

immediately to bring tidings of the Queen's death, and the
Governor had no option but to release Carter.

The story soon spread, much to the embarrassment of Sir
John, who was disliked by many Portsmouth officials. They
were only too pleased to add to his discomfort by saying slyly in
his presence, "Pray can you tell me if Queen Anne is dead?"

Ghosts
and Dragons

EVERY county has its ghost stories and Hampshire is well
endowed with tales of weird apparitions and strange
legends of the supernatural.

Phantom monks visit the ruins of Netley Abbey, and walk in
the ways of Beaulieu, while strange lights have been seen
hovering over the burial place of the nuns of Wherwell Abbey.
But one of the most anguished ghosts of Hampshire is that of a
cleric who roams Conholt Hill near Vernham Dean.

The village, at the far end of the Bourne Valley, was struck by
plague in 1666 and the Vicar, fearful of becoming a victim,
persuaded the villagers who were already stricken to go to the
top of the hill where they could stay in the Pest House. He
promised that if they would isolate themselves in this fashion for
the sake of the other villagers, he would take them food and
water. However, he then became so concerned for his own
safety that he neglected their welfare. Those who did not die
from the plague slowly died from starvation. But a just retri-
bution overtook him. In spite of all precautions, he finally
contracted the disease and died of it. The Vicar is said to
haunt the hill, a lonely figure who wanders in his clerical robes
along the path he should have taken to tend his unfortunate
parishioners.

A more pleasant story comes from Liphook where a horseman was riding home one night when he heard the sound of
flute-like music coming from an elm tree. He paused and looked

up into the tree to see who it was who made such magic music at that hour of night, but there was no sign of the flautist. The man rode on but soon became aware of a boy walking at his side, playing the flute. The traveller listened to the enchanting notes and then spoke to the boy but there was no answer, so he started to dismount to look more closely at his young companion. Suddenly something stretched across the roadway in front of the horseman, a long bramble he thought, but it brushed his hat over his eyes, and by the time he had straightened his headgear the boy, the bramble, and the music, had gone.

When the traveller spoke of his strange experience he found that others had seen and heard the boy – but that was over sixty years ago.

In Odiham, a grey lady flits from house to house. She was first seen one night by the wife of a coachman who worked at the George Inn. He sometimes returned home very late after taking his clients to their respective destinations, and his wife felt anxious as she waited for his return from what were often lonely rides. On this particular night she thought she heard him approaching the house and she hastened to the window. But as she held back the curtain she saw a phantom figure which walked straight through her fence and then continued in the direction of the churchyard.

It so terrified the coachman's wife that she begged her husband to give up his job at the George, and as soon as it could be arranged he took over a nearby alehouse so that his late night jaunts were over. The sceptical may think that the story was but a clever invention on the part of the good wife to keep her husband at home at nights, but the grey lady is reputed to have been seen by others, and for good measure, Odiham also has a lady dressed in black who flits about the fields outside the village.

I wonder what has happened to the Grey Lady of Netley now that the great military hospital is no more? She used to haunt the quarter-of-a-mile-long corridors, and the thought of meeting her made the night nurses hurry along those dimly-lit passages as they went from ward to ward to attend the patients.

The weirdest story of all Hampshire must come from Wherwell. Although a legend, it is certainly eerie enough to be included as a tale of the supernatural.

The legend tells of a duck who laid an egg in the crypt of the old Abbey. The egg was hatched by a toad and produced a cockatrice – a terrible dragon-like creature. When small it was regarded as an unusual pet and was well cared for by the villagers, but it grew into a monster that demanded human beings as part of its diet. It would fly over the countryside and swoop down upon its victims, then carry them off in its talons to its lair.

Something had to be done about the horrific creature and a reward of four acres of land was offered to any man who could rid the village of the cockatrice.

Several attempts were made to kill the creature but all failed and many lost their lives. At last a man named Green devised a clever scheme. He polished a piece of steel until it shone like a mirror, and lowered it into the monster's lair. The cockatrice thought that it had a rival when it saw its own reflection in the bright surface and immediately attacked. It battered itself against the steel until it became exhausted and Green was able to kill it with his long spear.

Thus the beautiful village of Wherwell was freed from the curse of the cockatrice, but duck's eggs were never again eaten by the villagers. And strangely enough there are four acres of Harewood Forest which are still known as Green's Acres!

Jack the Painter

B RITISH, Roman, and Saxon seafarers used the harbour at
Portsmouth long before the Norman king, Henry I, built
Porchester Castle on the ruins of an earlier Roman fortification.
He saw the need to defend the harbour and the port which stood
in so strategic a position on our coastline, and from those early
beginnings the great naval port we know today has developed
over the centuries.

The dockyard dates from the early sixteenth century, and
the great ships which have berthed there have thrown giant
shadows over the quayside. Any man who wished to avoid the
attention of the sentries at night could find ready cover in the
darkness beside the huge hulls.

One chill December night in 1776, Jack the Painter moved
cautiously along the dockside. He paused at the ropehouse and
then moved swiftly and silently into the darkness. Soon a
terrifying brightness glowed into the far corners of the yard as
flames devoured the ropehouse and then spread rapidly,
causing great damage before they were finally brought under
control.

Jack, or to give him his real name, John Aitken, fled from the
scene of his crime but he was later arrested in the Raven Inn at
Hook and was taken to Winchester to stand trial for arson.

It was found that the prisoner was born in Edinburgh in 1752
and had been apprenticed to a painter – hence his nickname.
He apparently tired of his trade and made his way to Gravesend

where he enlisted in the army at a time when recruits were needed for the war with America. He deserted, but thought better of this decision and re-enlisted, probably under the name of Hinde.

During his time in America Aitken became attracted to the republican ideology and on his return to England he thought to benefit the cause of American independence by setting fire to all the British dockyards. For this purpose he invented two types of "infernal machines", one of which he used to start the fire at Portsmouth.

His ideals led him to an early death for he was condemned to be hanged from a sixty-feet-high gallows, the mast of the *Arethusa*, by the main gate of Portsmouth dockyard. This sentence was duly carried out and after death his corpse was tarred and hung in chains from Blockhouse Point at the mouth of the harbour as a warning to other would-be arsonists. As the chains creaked on a windy day, stories of ghosts and demons grew up round "Painter's Point", but that is not the end of the story.

After several years the body was taken down by some sailors who took it to a tavern in Gosport. What a horrible scene it must have made as the sailors sat drinking in the smoky, reeking taproom with their grisly companion at their sides. As the drinking grew harder, the money ran shorter, and soon they were asking for credit from their landlord; but he demanded surety before he refilled their empty tankards. What did they offer? The bones of Jack the Painter! And they were accepted by the landlord. Surely the strangest bond ever given in pledge to an innkeeper.

This incident was commemorated by a ditty which was sung by many a sailor as he sat drinking his ale:

"Whose corpse by pondrous irons wrung
High up on Blockhouse Beach was hung,
And long to every tempest swung?
Why truly, Jack the Painter.

> Whose bones some years since taken down
> Were brought in curious way to town,
> And left in pledge for half a crown?
> Why truly, Jack the Painter."

One hundred and fifteen years after his execution a horrifying relic was to recall his story to the Victorians. One of his mummified fingers, fitted as a tobacco stopper, was sent to the Naval exhibition at Chelsea in 1891. Surely a shudder ran down those prim Victorian spines as they gazed upon that gruesome exhibit, and spoke in hushed tones of the exploits of Jack the Painter.

Dead Man's Plack

D EAD MAN'S PLACK is the rather sinister name of a monument which stands in Harewood Forest, near Andover. It was erected in 1835 to commemorate the place where a story of love, jealousy and hate finally resolved into murder, and before overwhelming remorse ended the tragic tale, another life was to be sacrificed at Corfe Castle in Dorset.

The Anglo-Saxon King Aedgar was already a widower and father of a young son named Edward, when he heard of the charms of the fair Aelfrida, daughter of Ordgar, Ealdorman of Devon. The King wanted to know more about the beautiful girl and sent Aethelwald, Ealdorman of Hampshire, to see if the reports he had heard were true. Aedgar said that if Aelfrida was truly that beautiful he desired to make her his wife, and entrusted the Earl to use his judgment and, if favourable, to speak of the King's proposal.

When Aethelwald met Aelfrida he realised that the stories of her great beauty had not been exaggerated. Unfortunately for him he fell deeply in love with her and could not summon strength to tell her of the King's offer of marriage. He reported to the King that her charms had been much over-rated, and then returned and married her himself.

Later, the King, probably suspicious because he had not been allowed to meet the Earl's new wife, paid a visit to their domain and naturally expected to see his hostess.

Aethelwald begged in vain that Aelfrida should disguise her beauty. The truth came out. She was furious when she realised that her husband's deception had lost her the opportunity of becoming the Queen and instead of hiding her charms she walked proudly before the King, making no secret of her liking for him. As he gazed upon her perfection he was filled with envy. He could not forgive the Earl for his duplicity and planned revenge. It is said that Aelfrida knew of his intentions and connived with him.

Aethelwald was soon invited to the King's house at Andover. One fine morning the King and Earl rode out together to hunt in Harewood Forest. At the place where the monument now stands, the King plunged a javelin into the Earl's back, mortally wounding him. He then promptly took the newly widowed Aelfrida for his queen.

During the next ten years she fulfilled her ambition to hold sway over the King's court, but when Aedgar died in 975 she saw her stepson Edward ascend his late father's throne. For four years she was consumed with jealousy as she watched the young king, for she longed to see her own son, Aethelred, in his place.

Just as King Aedgar had awaited his opportunity to rid himself of her first husband, so she now waited to dispose of her stepson. As they supped one night at Corfe Castle in the year 979 she passed him a stirrup cup and, under this token of goodwill, she stabbed him to death. Thus Aethelred the Unready took the throne from King Edward the Martyr and another page was turned in the history of England.

Aelfrida's ambition had been achieved through murder for the second time, but the cost proved too high, even for her. She was stricken by remorse and desperately sought a way to expiate her dreadful crimes. In 986 she founded a nunnery in the royal manor of Wherwell on the banks of the Test, and there she lived a life of penitence until her death in the year 1000.

The seasons have dealt kindly with the scenes associated with the crimes. Falling leaves have covered the blood-stained earth where Aethelwald fell, and young deer move quietly through the forest undergrowth.

Nothing of Aelfrida's nunnery remains except a few fragments of masonry, and the recumbent stone effigy of an abbess, now lying in the Wherwell Parish Church of St. Peter and Holy Cross. The silver waters of the Test flow past the site where once a queen tried to expunge her guilt, and time has dimmed the tragedy incited by her beauty.